Olga Lengyel, Auschwitz Survivor

Peter Davies · Hannah Holtschneider ·
Sheila E. Jelen · Christoph Thonfeld

Olga Lengyel, Auschwitz Survivor

Interdisciplinary Explorations

Peter Davies
University of Edinburgh
Edinburgh, UK

Sheila E. Jelen
University of Chicago
Chicago, IL, USA

Hannah Holtschneider
University of Edinburgh
Edinburgh, UK

Christoph Thonfeld
Dachau Concentration Camp
Memorial Site
Dachau, Germany

ISBN 978-3-031-82489-0   ISBN 978-3-031-82490-6   (eBook)
https://doi.org/10.1007/978-3-031-82490-6

This Palgrave Macmillan imprint is published by the registered company Springer Nature Switzerland AG
The registered company address is: Gewerbestrasse 11, 6330 Cham, Switzerland

If disposing of this product, please recycle the paper.

Acknowledgements

The writing of this book has been enabled and enriched by numerous people. We are grateful to Gabriel Finder for initiating our collaboration. We first presented aspects of our research at the following conferences: *The Future of Holocaust Testimonies* (Western Galilee College, 2019), *Life-Writing in Times of Crisis* (IABA, Warsaw, 2023) and *Lessons & Legacies* (Prague, 2023). Borbála Klacsmann and András Széczény helped with translations from the Hungarian. Beatrix Futák-Campbell made the Hungarian translation of Olga Lengyel's testimony available and Bess Dawson assisted with translation queries. Paul Parvis contributed an invaluable explanation of Catholic understandings of *mea culpa*. Sebastian Paul, Andrea Rudorff, Debórah Dwork and Sue Vice were wonderful interlocutors at various stages of our project. We are grateful to the United States Holocaust Memorial Museum for the permission to reproduce the map of Hungary, HEROMAX for the use of the map of Auschwitz-Birkenau and Akiva Himelhoch for annotating it in English to our specifications. The Leverhulme Trust, the University of Kentucky, the Bavarian Memorial Foundation and the University of Edinburgh provided generous support for our work. An early and much abbreviated version of Sheila Jelen's essay appeared in the Association for Jewish Studies magazine, *Perspectives* (Winter 2023) under the title, 'An Improbable Likeness: Olga Lengyel's Auschwitz Tale of Motherhood Lost'.

CONTENTS

About the Authors

Peter Davies is Professor of Modern German Studies at the University of Edinburgh, UK. His research is concerned with the intersection of Translation Studies and Holocaust Studies methods and with the significance of translation and interpreting for the development of Holocaust memory. He is the author of *Witness between Languages: The Translation of Holocaust Testimony in Context* (Boydell & Brewer, 2018), and is co-editor with Jean-Boase-Beier, Andrea Hammel and Marion Winters, of *Translating Holocaust Lives* (Bloomsbury, 2018). He has also published on issues of translation in the work of Elie Wiesel, Tadeusz Borowski, Krystyna Żywulska and Yitzhak Katzenelson and has written on the work of Bertha Pappenheim and Anselm Kiefer. He is currently working on a study entitled *Interpreting at the First Frankfurt Auschwitz Trial: How is a Witness Heard?*

Hannah Holtschneider is Professor of Contemporary Jewish Cultural History at the University of Edinburgh, UK. She is a cultural historian of twentieth-century Jewish history, with a particular focus on the consequences of the Holocaust, Jewish identities and Jewish/non-Jewish relations. She is the author of three monographs *Jewish Orthodoxy in Scotland: Rabbi Dr Salis Daiches and Religious Leadership* (EUP 2019), *The Holocaust and Representations of Jews: History and Identity in the Museum* (Routledge 2011), *German Protestants Remember the Holocaust: Theology and the Construction of Collective Memory* (Lit. Verlag 2001) and numerous articles. She is currently working on a family correspondence of Jewish refugees from Kassel.

Sheila E. Jelen is Professor of Religion, Literature and Visual Culture and The History of Judaism in the Divinity School at the University of Chicago. Prior to this appointment, she was the Zantker Professor of Jewish Literature, Culture and History at the University of Kentucky, Lexington and the director of the Jewish Studies Program there. She is the author of *Israeli Salvage Poetics* (2023) exploring the ways in which Israeli writers and scholars have represented East European Jewish life in their work from the 1930s to the present, *Salvage Poetics: American-Jewish Post-Holocaust Folk Ethnographies* (2020) and *Intimations of Difference: Dvora Baron in the Modern Hebrew Renaissance* (2007). She has edited numerous volumes, including *Reconstructing the Old Country: American Jewry in the Post-Holocaust Decades* (2017), *Modern Jewish Literatures: Intersections and Boundaries* (2011) and *Hebrew, Gender, and Modernity* (2007). Her most recent book, *Testimonial Montage: A Family of Holocaust Testimonies from the Cracow Ghetto Resistance* (2024) considers, through a literary lens, the testimonies of a group of Israeli Holocaust survivors who were active in the Cracow ghetto uprising.

Christoph Thonfeld is a historian and has done research and/or taught at Bremen University, Hagen University and Trier University (all in Germany), at Cheng Chi University and National Taiwan Normal University (both in Taiwan/ROC) and at University College London (UK). Currently, he is the head of the research department at the Dachau Concentration Camp Memorial Site in Germany. His main areas of interest are twentieth-century German and European history, especially the Nazi era and its aftermath (Nazi crimes trials and media coverage, remembrance of the Nazi past, changes in Holocaust survivor testimony over time), Oral History and Memory Studies. He has authored three monographs: *Normalisierung des Außergewöhnlichen. Der Wandel der Erinnerungskultur des Zweiten Weltkriegs und des Holocaust in Deutschland 1990–2010*, Taipei 2015; *Rehabilitierte Erinnerungen? Individuelle Erfahrungsverarbeitung und kollektive Repräsentationen von NS-Zwangsarbeit im internationalen Vergleich*, Essen 2014; and *Sozialkontrolle und Eigensinn. Denunziation am Beispiel Thüringens 1933–1949*, Cologne/Weimar/Vienna 2003.

LIST OF FIGURES

CHAPTER 1

Olga Lengyel, Auschwitz Survivor: Contexts

Peter Davies, Hannah Holtschneider, Sheila E. Jelen,
and Christoph Thonfeld

Abstract The introduction sets out what we know about Olga Lengyel's life and her multiple testimonies. The chapter then outlines the field of research into multiple testimonies and the study of gender in relation to the Holocaust, as well as provides a historical context about the Auschwitz-Birkenau camp complex and trials of Nazi crimes after the end of World War II.

Keywords Testimony · Gender · Auschwitz · Nazi crimes · Trials · Hungary

This publication arises from a long series of conversations about one of the most intriguing, but still under-researched, aspects of Holocaust testimony: how the remembering and telling of an individual survivor changes through time, through shifting contexts and with increasing age. Our aim is not to produce a single overarching narrative or interpretation, but to come at this issue from an interdisciplinary perspective to explore how analyses of the same texts performed by scholars in different disciplines overlap, conflict with, or complement each other.

Long-term studies of a single survivor's development as a witness are still rare. Testimony is more often read for other purposes: as historical

P. Davies et al., *Olga Lengyel, Auschwitz Survivor*,
https://doi.org/10.1007/978-3-031-82490-6_1

evidence, or as a basis for reflections on subjective experience, language and the possibility or impossibility of communication. A small number of prominent survivors, such as Elie Wiesel, Primo Levi, Charlotte Delbo and others, can be considered to have produced a 'life's work' in testimony: but these survivors are 'writers' in the modern, Western sense of the word, as well as witnesses, so their work is also read in literary-critical terms, exploring the link between personality, biography and work.

Of course, most survivors are not 'writers' in this sense. Many published nothing and never spoke in public beyond either their family or their solidarity groups; we should not forget that any witness who produces even one published testimony statement—whether written or spoken—is an exception. Nevertheless, there are still many extraordinary individuals whose public careers as witnesses may be as long-lasting and complex as those of Levi or Wiesel: multifaceted, encompassing multiple genres, addressing various audiences, remarkably consistent or richly contradictory. They are not, however, often thought of as producing a 'body of work' that should be considered as a whole, the individual parts set in relation both to each other and to the context of their articulation.

Several excellent studies have taken a longitudinal view of the way a survivor works through their experiences, such as *Approaching an Auschwitz Survivor: Holocaust Testimony and Its Transformations*, the empathetic historical exploration of the testimonies of Helen Tichauer edited by Jürgen Matthäus (Matthäus 2009)[1] or works by Michael Pollak and colleagues (Pollak et al. 2016) and Christopher Browning (Browning 2003). However, these studies tend to take a single disciplinary perspective through the eyes of one scholar. Our approach is different, not trying to find unity in a variety or to impose a single form of reading and listening but allowing the contrasts between our perspectives to become part of our inquiry and to explore the insights that arise from this practice. We are two historians, a translation expert, and a literature scholar. In this volume we draw from our distinct methodologies and disciplines to cross-fertilise one another's approaches to Holocaust testimonies in general, and to one series of Holocaust testimonies in particular.

Longitudinal approaches to listening to and working with survivors over time and participating in this way in the production of a testimony

---

[1] This book was an at least indirect corollary of the first systematic attempt at re-interviewing survivors by USHMM. Cf. https://collections.ushmm.org/search/catalog/irn44522 (accessed 31 May 2024).

through dialogue, as pioneered by Laub and Greenspan in the tradition of oral history, have been a defining influence (Plato, Leh, and Thonfeld 2010; Greenspan 2010a; 2010b, 2015). Nevertheless, this intimate and productive form of communication between survivor and researcher is a privilege that is not available to all and requires specific training and set of methods. There is much to learn here about the listener's involvement and ethical responsibilities and the rhythmic unfolding of a testimony through time, but we also need to find ways of understanding the testimonies of survivors who are no longer available to interview, or perhaps prefer to produce finished, published statements than to engage in open-ended dialogue.

We have chosen to think about the testimonies of Olga Lengyel: her witness statements have not attained the status of the works by Wiesel, Delbo or Levi, but she is still well enough known to have gained a public profile as an educator and philanthropist. Her testimonies have, indeed, attracted both a wide audience and some scholarly attention, including doubts that have been raised about her testimonies. These present persistent and challenging questions for us to address as scholars.

Lengyel's published memoir is one of the very earliest post-war testimonies, coming out in French in 1946 and English a year later; much later in her life, in 1998, she gave a video interview to the USC Shoah Foundation Visual History Archive. Her work is internationally known, has been translated and received in a number of languages and inspired William Styron's bestselling novel *Sophie's Choice* (Styron 2010 [originally published in 1979]; see 1997, 396). Her testimony as a Hungarian Jewish woman from Transylvania with medical training, who survived Auschwitz as a medical orderly in the Jewish women's infirmary in Birkenau, has played a key role in scholarship about the experiences of female victims of the Nazis and in controversies about truth, truthfulness, embellishment and falsehood in testimony. Our contributions to this volume address all of these vital issues in different ways. Our study concentrates on her published testimonies, written and oral, rather than on private correspondence, as we are interested in her public self-positioning and the way she occupies and performs the role of survivor-witness.

In what follows, we will provide an overview of Lengyel's life and the history of her testimonies. Then we will present four contexts for better understanding the variety of approaches we take towards this distinct body of testimonies and their trajectory over time. The first context situates our work within the field of varying approaches to Holocaust testimonies over the last half a century. This is followed by two contexts that are primarily historical, focused on the history of Auschwitz/Birkenau and on the post-war trials of Nazi crimes, with an emphasis on Lengyel's relationship to each. The fourth context explores the study of gendered experiences in the Holocaust.

OLGA LENGYEL: BIOGRAPHICAL NOTES

As will become clear, Lengyel rewrote and retold details of her biography throughout her life. Most of the information we have about Lengyel's biography comes from her own narratives. While there is corroborating evidence for many of the events she describes, there are elements that recur in her telling that have to be taken for granted. We interpret these varying narratives in different ways, depending on our disciplinary and methodological perspectives, so we do not view it as our role to establish a strictly objective biographical truth against which to judge the varying story elements that Lengyel musters throughout her life. Nevertheless, it will be useful to provide a bare-bones outline of her biography, as far as it can be established, for the sake of context, to avoid repetition in the individual chapters and to provide something for the reader to refer back to. We acknowledge where there are gaps and doubts but leave the work of interpretation to the individual chapters.

To understand Lengyel's self-expression, we need to be aware of the social context of her early life, which placed her in the maelstrom of the Holocaust in Hungary following occupation by Nazi Germany in March 1944. The Holocaust in Hungary unfolded in the spring and summer of 1944, a few brief months during which the majority of Hungary's c.800,000 Jews were murdered (Fig. 1.1).[2]

Never having lived anywhere other than in Kolozsvár/Cluj, Lengyel was nevertheless at home in three different states before deportation to Auschwitz-Birkenau in May 1944. She was born in 1908 in the Hungarian Kingdom of the Austro-Hungarian Monarchy (1867–1918), resided in Romania from 1920 to 1940, then again in Hungary until it was occupied by Nazi Germany on 19 March 1944.[3] Like many of

---

[2] For an overview of research on the Holocaust in Hungary see Braham and Kovács (2016); Braham and Miller (1998); for the Holocaust in Transylvania in particular see Tibori Szabó (2016).

[3] For an overview of Hungarian Jewish history see Patai (2015).

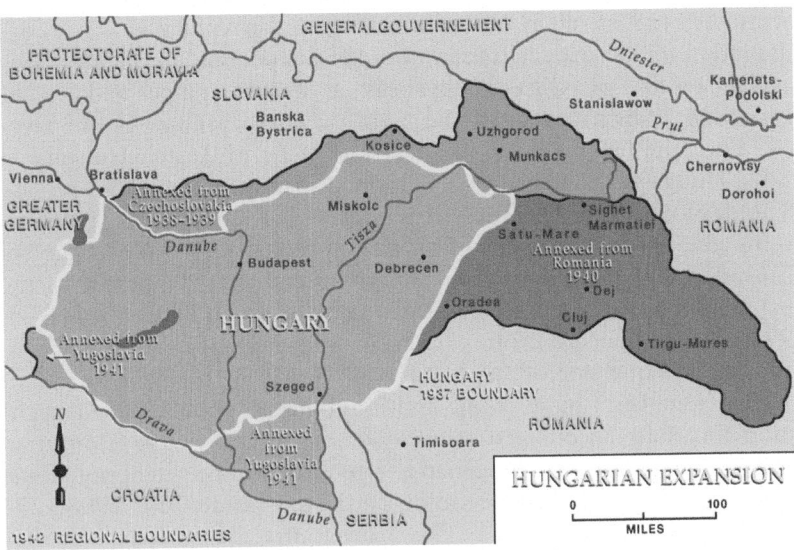

Fig. 1.1 Map of Hungary in 1944. Reproduced with the kind permission of the United States Holocaust Memorial Museum

her origin and social class, Lengyel grew up multi-lingual. She consistently presents herself as part of the Hungarian-speaking majority culture of Cluj. In her video interview in 1998, she refers to the city only by its Hungarian name Kolozsvár. Her education included instruction in German, French and English, recognising German as the other dominant language of the Austro-Hungarian Monarchy, showing cultural affinity to her extended family in France and evidencing a cosmopolitan orientation by her family employing an English governess. Lengyel does not reference any competence in Romanian, even though as a result of the post-World War I political reordering of Europe, Cluj belonged to Romania during a formative period of her youth. Lengyel also does not speak Yiddish— for centuries the *lingua franca* of East Central European Jewry—and she eschews any identification with religion, only reluctantly acknowledging her Jewish origins in her 1998 Shoah Foundation interview, having not mentioned this at all in her memoir.[4] She also continually expresses admiration for German culture in both her memoir and in the interview.

This profile of Olga Lengyel as a wealthy, upper-middle-class Hungarian Jewish woman in the early twentieth century is not atypical. Since the beginning of the dual monarchy of Austria-Hungary in 1867, Hungarian Jews enjoyed full emancipation, permitting entry to all professions and all sections of Hungarian society. Indeed, Hungary during the Austro-Hungarian Monarchy ushered in a 'golden age' of Hungarian Jewish relations that came to an end with the demise of the dual monarchy at the end of World War I (Mendelsohn 2001, 95; Braham 1998, 27). Nineteenth-century Hungary's strong policy of 'Magyarisation' was an expression of the notion of an 'expansive nation' that sought to bring together a multi-ethnic and multi-lingual population. Magyarisation forcefully encouraged minority-ethnic groups in the Hungarian Monarchy to identify as Hungarian and to abandon their minority-ethnic language and culture (Mendelsohn 2001, 87–94; Braham 1998, 27–28; Tibori Szabó 2016, 147). This proved attractive to Jews who thus gained access to all parts of Hungarian society, in contrast to other European countries, not least the Austrian part of the dual monarchy, where Jews continued to suffer social and economic disadvantages throughout the long nineteenth century. As a result, the majority of the Hungarian Jewish population understood themselves as Hungarian, spoke Hungarian as their native language and fully assimilated into Hungarian society, regarding themselves as 'Hungarians of the Mosaic faith' (Mendelsohn 2001, 92; Braham 1998, 40–41). Hungarian Jews, particularly in urban areas, were more similar to German Jews in their linguistic and cultural assimilation, than they were to other Eastern European Jews whose social and political experiences did not lead to full-scale assimilation.

Lengyel was the daughter of industrialist Ferdinánd Bernát-Bernard, director of coal mining in Transylvania, and of Ileana Légmán who was involved in charitable work. This places her firmly in the 'industrial and commercial bourgeoisie' (Mendelsohn 2001, 92), well-connected among her social peers and, as she presents herself, at the heart of a number of institutions in the city, such as her husband's sanatorium and her mother's

---

[4] Indeed, commentators signal uncertainty whether she was Jewish (Styron 1997, 396) and one of our interlocutors for this volume pursued the question in depth and asked in a conference paper, 'Was Olga Lengyel Jewish?' (Finder, IABA Warsaw 2023, https://iabawarsaw2023.eu/schedule [accessed 21 March 2024]).

work at a local orphanage. While rural Transylvanian Jewry was among the least assimilated and most traditionally religious and often poor, Jews in the city of Kolozsvár were also part of an urban assimilated elite (see Turda 2016, 75; and Case 2007). Lengyel never describes her upbringing in terms of Jewish religious observance, culture, language or traditions. Indeed, she appears to have attended a Catholic girls' school (Turda 2016, 74). It is not clear how much Lengyel's family was involved with the religious Jewish communities, though her 1998 interview mentions her father's involvement as a donor and host in the community and that the family observed Jewish festivals.

Lengyel's husband, Dr. Miklós Lengyel, was a surgeon and gynaecologist with a clinic in Cluj. Although she initially had studied for a degree in literature, Lengyel trained to be his surgical assistant and they jointly ran the clinic. The couple had two sons: her memoir names them as Thomas and Arvad, while her 1998 Shoah Foundation testimony refers to one as Thomas Arvad and the other as David, who, in her 1998 testimony, Lengyel claims was adopted.[5]

The destiny of the Lengyel family in the Holocaust was intimately connected to the geopolitics of the region beginning during the interwar period. The increasing political alignment of Hungary with the Axis powers in the 1930s, under the leadership of Regent Admiral Miklós Horthy (1920–1944), saw Hungary regain territory ceded in the aftermath of World War I. The Second Vienna Award in 1940 restored Transylvania—and with it Kolozsvár/Cluj—to Hungary (see also Case 2007). Many Hungarian Jews at first saw their re-entry into Hungary as a positive development that released them from the recent antisemitic legislation introduced by Romania (Tibori Szabó 2016, 148–49). This relief was short-lived as the reality of antisemitic persecution sunk in:

Between 1940 and 1944, during Hungarian rule, Northern Transylvanian Jewry were exposed to several waves of atrocities: firstly, to expulsion and deportation to Galicia; secondly, to the 'Holocaust by bullets'; thirdly, to extermination by work, hunger, and disease during the forced labor service;

[5] The spelling of her sons' names varies between different editions, reflecting the norms of the language of the edition. The recent Hungarian edition (Lengyel and Stier 2021, 10) restores Hungarian spelling (Tamás and Árvád). Given that there is some variance in their names between Lengyel's testimonies, it is hard to state with certainty that this is the 'original' spelling, so we have used the names as they appear in the edition we are referring to.

and, finally, to the mass deportation to Auschwitz and the almost total destruction in German Nazi camps. (Tibori Szabó 2016, 149)[6]

The situation of Hungarian Jewry considerably worsened in March 1944 when Nazi Germany occupied Hungary to prevent a Hungarian peace agreement with the Western Allies. This occupation spelled deportation and murder for Jews residing in Hungary who had suffered years of antisemitic discrimination and exclusion from civil society but had largely been protected from deportation until then. Between May and July 1944 at least 437,000 Jews from across Hungary were deported to Auschwitz-Birkenau.

Lengyel's testimonies in 1946/7 and 1998 include passages relating her deliberations about accompanying her husband on the transport in May 1944. The following account by Tibori Szabó suggests that she may have been referring here to intentional misinformation spread by Hungarian authorities, in order to quell suspicion among the Jewish population:

> In the meantime, the authorities spread the information that the 'Jewish workers' who were supposed to be sent to Germany would be allowed to be accompanied by their families. They did this in order to increase their feelings of safety and to maximize their working performance within the enterprises of the German war industry. This information was also enforced by very cynical statements of Sztójay and Horthy. (Tibori Szabó 2016, 166)

Additionally, Lengyel recalled her own and her husband's positive past views of interwar German society, which she struggled to reconcile with the Germany that brought about her ordeal in Auschwitz-Birkenau. In this way, she tried to convey to the reader how the Germans' deception techniques were so successful that even she was fatally deceived. In the 1998 interview, she was more open with her condemnation of both Hungarians and Germans as far as their support for and collaboration with the Nazi regime are concerned. On a declaratory level at least, she was then able to lay the blame for her relatives' deaths firmly on the Germans who were 'elegantly dressed', 'lied all the time', (Part I, 1h26min) and

---

[6] See also Eisen (2023) for an exploration of the Holocaust by bullets in Transylvania.

'abused her [Lengyel's] trust' (Part I, 1h34min). Her much more elaborate version of how the destruction of her family unfolded as a result of her husband's alleged anti-German activities amid widespread local Hungarian collaboration with the Germans (Part I, 1h22min) does not appear in the published versions of her book.

In a 1994 affidavit given for Rabbi Dr. Moshe Carmilly, who was rabbi to the Neolog Jewish community of Kolozsvár and who from 1941 to 44 helped Jewish refugees from Nazi-occupied countries cross the border to nearby Romania, Lengyel suggests that she and her husband contributed to these rescue efforts and that they were urged to flee themselves (Carmilly-Weinberger 1994, 178).[7] They decided against this due to Olga's father being sick, and thus were deported with the remainder of the Jewish population of Cluj to Auschwitz-Birkenau (Carmilly-Weinberger 1994, 178). Olga and Miklós survived the selection at Birkenau, but her parents and their sons were sent to the gas chamber straight away, along with the majority of the arrivals (Tibori Szabó 2016, 170). Olga worked, for a time, in the Jewish women's infirmary in Birkenau, while Miklós was sent to the Buna subcamp, where he worked as a medical orderly; she claims to have been able to visit him briefly in Buna before he died.

Lengyel's testimony is remembered for its forceful account of the work of Jewish women doctors in Birkenau and the devastating moral choices they had to make in choosing how to save pregnant women. It is also known, at least in its English version, for its description of the sado-masochistic cruelty of SS guards, especially the notorious female guard Irma Grese. In our individual chapters, Sheila E. Jelen discusses the relationship of her text to other memoirs by Jewish women doctors and Christoph Thonfeld and Peter Davies explore, from different perspectives, her depiction of perpetrators.

Lengyel also claims to have been recruited to the camp resistance by a French prisoner she refers to as L., working for them as a courier and helping to prepare the Birkenau *Sonderkommando* uprising of 7 October

---

[7] This speaks both to their Jewish identification, but also to their philanthropic commitments. The former is a matter of some contention in light of Lengyel's reluctance to acknowledge her Jewishness publicly, while the latter is a powerful motif throughout her narrative of survival, and in the post-war period when she established a foundation dedicated to educating the world about the Holocaust (https://www.toli.us/ [accessed 21 March 2024]).

1944. Her account of liberation varies. She describes being saved from a death march by Polish villagers in January 1945 and sheltering there until the Red Army arrived, after which she moved to Paris to stay with a cousin, László Légman, mingling with other survivors and members of her extended family. We have evidence that she met a former French resistance fighter, Maurice Lequeux (presumably 'L.') (McNeish 2007, 163, 166), in March 1945 in Lublin, just before she moved to Paris, and that she followed the Bergen-Belsen trial, held by the British in the autumn of 1945.[8] Christoph Thonfeld discusses the significance of these events in his chapter.

Lengyel spent approximately two years in Paris, from 1945 to 47, before she emigrated to the United States. In her USC Shoah Foundation interview, she reports that her cousin László Légman supported her initially, but that she then lived independently and wrote her memoir first published in 1946 as *Souvenirs de l'au-delà* (Memoirs from the Beyond). How she supported herself is less clear, but we do know that on emigration to the United States, Lengyel took with her the family's art collection which her father had deposited in Paris during the 1930s.[9] Therefore, she may have had independent means, suggesting that we should not imagine her as impoverished in the way many survivors were. It is also not clear whether she interacted with the transitional refugee community that was supported by the Jewish community in Paris.[10] We also do not know whether she (re-)connected with fellow Hungarian Jewish Auschwitz prisoner, Dr. Gisella Perl[11] while both were staying in Paris (Rudorff 2020, 9).

While we cannot build a good picture of the social scene in which Lengyel moved in Paris, we can deduce that she must have been in touch with Jewish immigrants who came to Paris between the world wars. One such significant contact was Ladislas Gara, a Hungarian Jewish

---

[8] Lengyel refers to Lequeux as 'L.' in her book and names him as Lequeux in her Shoah Foundation interview in 1998.

[9] See *Le Quotidien de l'art* (2015); see also D'Arcy (2015).

[10] For assistance available to Jewish refugees in post-war France see Schpun (2010); for a broader discussion of Jewish life in post-war France see Hand and Katz (2015).

[11] Dr. Perl (1907–1988) was a Transylvanian Jewish obstetrician who was enslaved as a doctor in the Jewish women's infirmary in Birkenau at the same time as Olga Lengyel. Lengyel refers to Perl as Dr. G. throughout her memoir. Perl's memoir *I was a Doctor in Auschwitz* was first published in 1948.

journalist and writer from Budapest who had settled in France in the mid-1920s, having been refused entry to university in Hungary in the early 1920s due to quotas on Jewish students. Alongside publishing his own work, Gara quickly gained a reputation as a translator from Hungarian to French, whereby he became an ambassador for Hungarian literature in France. During the German occupation, Gara and his wife Nathalie moved in resistance circles and collaborated on a novel about Jewish refugees arriving in a small French town (*St Boniface et ses juifs* (The Jews of St Boniface): Éditions du Bateau Ivre, 1946). Gara, we can surmise from the French edition of Lengyel's memoir, was somehow involved in the translation and adaptation of Lengyel's text, paving the way towards publication for a hitherto unknown author. The inclusion of the French Christian poet Pierre Emmanuel's 1945 poem *Hymne pour le retour des captifs* (Anthem for the return of the captives)[12] in the opening pages of *Souvenirs de l'au-delà* signals that Lengyel must have been introduced to circles that supported and made possible the publication of her book.

By 1947, she had moved to New York, where she published an English edition of her book.[13] We do not have much detail about her post-war activities, but we know that she married a man called Gustavo Aguire and moved with him to Cuba, where they had property and housed her significant art collection.[14]

These possessions were expropriated by the Castro regime after the Cuban Revolution (1953–59) and Lengyel returned to New York, where she lived for the rest of her life. Documentation of the United States Cuban Claims Commission relating to claims for restitution, following the revival by President Trump of sanctions under the Clinton-era Helms-Burton Act, shows the property in Havana in her name to a value of $4,865,766.48; this puts her among the very wealthiest US property-holders on the island, alongside many corporate interests.[15] The claim to restitution was revived by her estate in 2015.[16]

---

[12] First published Emmanuel (1945).

[13] We set out the publication and translation history in detail in the next section.

[14] See https://www.toli.us/about/olga-lengyel/ (accessed 31 May 2024).

[15] https://www.justice.gov/sites/default/files/fcsc/pages/attachments/2014/12/18/cuban_basic_claimant_info_value.pdf, 1 (accessed 12 February 2024).

[16] See D'Arcy (2015).

In New York, Lengyel followed in the footsteps of her mother, continuing the tradition of socially and culturally engaged philanthropy characteristic of determined, educated women from the European *haute-bourgeoisie*. In his chapter, Christoph Thonfeld refers to her as a 'philanthropist educational entrepreneur', who founded in New York the Memorial Library and Art Collection of the Second World War, which later became The Olga Lengyel Institute for Holocaust Studies and Human Rights (https://www.toli.us/). She died in April 2001.

OLGA LENGYEL'S TESTIMONIES

Lengyel is best known to Anglophone readers for her written testimony, now published under the title *Five Chimneys: A Woman Survivor's True Story of Auschwitz*, and for a videotaped interview she gave to the USC Shoah Foundation in 1998. For this study, we have settled on the most readily available English edition of her text as our common point of reference; it is also the latest English edition published while Lengyel was still alive. Unless stated otherwise, all references will be to this edition (Lengyel 2000).

The status of this edition of *Five Chimneys* as a point of reference should not disguise the fact that the text itself is unstable and varied, having gone through a complex process of rewriting, editing, translation, excerpting and collaboration. It has this in common with many testimony texts, especially the very early ones, that were published in a time of post-war upheaval, financial difficulty, uncertain publication opportunities, varying audience expectations and doubt about what testimony is and should be. This issue is discussed in more detail and from different perspectives in all of the chapters to follow, but we set out here for reference a brief summary of different editions and translations, as far as could be established.

The manuscript written by Olga Lengyel in either or both Hungarian and French seems to be either lost or, at least, no longer publicly available. Lengyel's first published testimony statement appeared in Paris in 1946 as *Souvenirs de l'au-delà* (Lengyel 1946), published by Éditions du Bateau Ivre. The next year, an English version came out in the United States under two different titles, by the same publisher, Ziff Davis: *Five Chimneys: The Story of Auschwitz* and *I Survived Hitler's Ovens* (Lengyel 1947a; b). A further edition with the title *I Survived Hitler's Ovens* was published in 1957 (Lengyel 1957), but from the 1970s, the text became available under a slightly modified version of the other English title *Five Chimneys: A Woman Survivor's True Story of Auschwitz*.[17] The English text has been in print continuously, but the French edition is no longer available. An edition in Lengyel's native Hungarian, translated from the English text by Ágnes Stier, was published in 2021 (Lengyel and Stier 2021).

The English and French editions are not identical: the English edition contains extra material and a different concluding chapter and some passages are expressed and structured differently. The French text opens with a lengthy poem by the resister Pierre Emmanuel, *Hymne pour le retour des captifs*, which is absent from the English. The English editions we have seen always open with a quotation from Albert Einstein, from a letter to the author: 'You have done a real service by letting the ones who are now silent and most forgotten speak'. Lengyel also used material from the English testimony for publications in men's magazines that were looking for salacious and dramatic stories from the concentration camps (Lengyel 1959). We can only speculate about the reasons for this, but the date of publication may suggest a need for financial security after the loss of her property in Cuba, or a way of marketing her book.

Extracts from her French testimony were published in important early collections of testimonies by survivors of Auschwitz put together by French survivor groups, probably indicating that she was well networked in these organisations (Bloch 1946; Wormser and Michel 1955). Multiple short extracts were published by Hermann Langbein in his account of Auschwitz based on survivor testimony, *Menschen in Auschwitz* (available in English as *People in Auschwitz*) (Langbein 1972; Langbein and Zohn 2004), but there has never been a full German translation of Lengyel's testimony.

In 1998, at a very different stage of her life, Lengyel recorded a lengthy testimony with the USC Shoah Foundation.[18] As Sheila E. Jelen,

---

[17] Throughout this book, quotes are taken from Olga Lengyel 2000, *Five Chimneys. A Woman Survivor's True Story of Auschwitz*. That edition also now contains a dedication 'to the memory of my parents and husband, my godfather and my children and to my fellow inmates of Hitler's concentration camps in World War Two who, silenced for ever, are mostly forgotten', presumably added by Olga Lengyel in 1959.

[18] Olga Lengyel Bernat-Bernard interviewed by Nancy Fisher on 28 August 1998. This testimony interview is available in full online. Part I https://youtu.be/ufxLw-xSEMM?si=WKRsYRUQhuwGkszR and Part II https://youtu.be/Zq1Uh_BiMso?si=M60jDwuu3mYTRKTI (accessed 15 January 2024).

Christoph Thonfeld and Hannah Holtschneider discuss in their chapters, Lengyel's approach to narrating her life story and the details that are important to her, differ in significant ways in this late testimony statement. She emphasises varying aspects of her family history, including denying that she married again after the war; she structures her account of the deportation, life in the camp and liberation in different ways, hinting at other elements of traumatic experience.

We have presented here an outline of her life and testimonies that can form the basis for further discussion and interpretation. The variations in the telling throughout her life are not unusual and thinking about them is one of the aims of this study. As we show in the course of this book, challenges have been made to the veracity of aspects of her story and we acknowledge the ethical problems that arise when thinking about testimony in terms of truth and falsehood, authenticity and trustworthiness. However, our aim is neither to demolish nor defend Lengyel's telling of her story; instead, we all take different perspectives on how to interpret gaps or contradictions in the context of the testimonies' articulation and are not interested in presenting one version against all the others as true.

In the rest of this Introduction, we set out some scholarly and historical context and our shared methodological ground. In the conclusion to the book, we pick up these threads again and explore how critics have read and listened to testimonies, including those of Olga Lengyel, as a way of testing and negotiating issues of truth and truthfulness, 'false' and 'embellished' testimony (see Vice 2014) and the marginalisation of the experiences of female victims.

Contexts

Research into Multiple Testimonies

The first survivor testimonies were already given while the murder of the Jews in Europe was still ongoing. Escapees from death camps, forced labour camps, concentration camps and deportation trains tried to pass on what they had experienced and seen in the forms of written texts and personal talks. Members of the *Sonderkommandos* in Auschwitz-Birkenau left behind harrowing descriptions, underground archives such as Oneg Shabbat collected witness evidence and across Eastern Europe Jewish historical commissions were established wherever the German army and occupation authorities were driven out. Immediately after the war, these early witnessing efforts continued on a collective level in DP camps and evolving survivor communities,[19] while individual survivors wrote memoirs to reach out to a larger audience, often with the intention of speaking on behalf of those who could no longer do so.

Psychologist and oral historian Henry Greenspan has explored the individual dynamics behind those early efforts and found that many survivors struggled with their uncertainty over whether they would find a receptive and understanding audience. Among numerous survivors, there was an initial 'urge to talk' to 'let the world know'. However, in the process they had to overcome fears of disbelief and indifference from their immediate social environment and societies at large. Since the late 1940s, this anxiety gave way to changing priorities of both, survivors and surrounding societies. They needed to re-establish their lives after a war which had afflicted most of them profoundly and to leave memories of the past behind. Consequently, survivors entered into what Greenspan has called the 'period of public silence' that lasted more than a decade or even into the late 1970s. To emphasise this caesura, he highlighted that 'there were more survivor memoirs published between 1945 and 1947 than during any three-year period until the end of the 1970s' (Greenspan 2000, 3–6). Lengyel's 1946 *Souvenirs de l'au-delà* and her 1947 *Five Chimneys* were part of this early peak. The English version never went dormant in the way others did but rather saw several reprints. In that context, Greenspan reminds us that many of these writings were not solely created by a solitary writer, but 'before writing, there was talk', more often among fellow survivors (Greenspan 2010b, 416). Although in her 1998 interview, Lengyel emphasised loneliness and nightmares as prominent post-war experiences, we can at least infer that exchanges about her ordeal at Auschwitz-Birkenau also took place during that time.

In the 1960s, with a number of high-profile Nazi crimes trials which gave many survivors a forum to speak publicly about their suffering, Annette Wieviorka saw the inception of the 'era of the witness' (Wieviorka 2006) which shifted the discourse of and research into the Holocaust.

---

[19] See, for example, the interview project of Jewish Latvian-American psychologist David Boder. On Boder's interview project see *Voices of the Holocaust* (Illinois Institute of Technology, 2009/2021), https://voices.library.iit.edu/ (accessed 2 March 2024). For an account of early efforts of survivors documenting their experiences and the history of their communities see Jockusch (2012).

While the criminal trials certainly gave more prominence to survivor-witness voices than at any time before, survivors also had to recalibrate their public accounts to fit in with the format of witness questioning (Weigel 2023, 42). This new public face of survivor perspectives, however, was modest in comparison to the remarkable visibility of these survivors beginning in the 1980s.

During the 1970s, incisive developments paved the way for a return to the prominence of Holocaust survivors' accounts of their suffering. After the disaster of the Vietnam War, the United States tried to reawaken the memories of the 'Good (World) War (II)' they had fought (Doßmann 2022, 245) which could be authenticated by survivors' stories of the German-led atrocities during that war. Israel needed to reclaim moral high ground after the Six Day and Yom Kippur Wars (1967 and 1973) against the internationally popular narrative of Palestinian liberation: a high ground which could be underscored by recollections of Jewish suffering. Moreover, in the Federal Republic of Germany a new generation was finally able and willing to look into the myriad stories of local perpetration against local victims in the 1930/40 s which had included a large number of Jews. The increasing awareness of the decline of the main generation of survivors was fuelled by the global popularity of the US TV series *Holocaust* (1978) and, in turn, inspired large-scale video documentation projects of survivors' accounts.[20] Additionally, these projects 'were a way to counter the earlier discounting of individual memory in historiography' (Greenspan et al. 2014, 195).

Those documentations of recounted individual experiences also led to an acknowledgement of survivors' exclusive and authentic knowledge of the experience of atrocities inflicted by Nazi Germany and its auxiliaries. It was this constellation that turned '"giving testimony" as an action' into an institutionalised reality and led to the emergence of the 'survivor-witness as a cultural type' (Greenspan et al. 2014, 193, 203). Already during that phase, a number of survivors who had been interviewed in the immediate post-war era testified again in very different circumstances, and often without reference to their previous testimony. The concept of testimony has found different interpretations ever since. Psychoanalyst Dori Laub understood it as a single comprehensive co-creative act between the

---

[20] For example, the Fortunoff Video Archive For Holocaust Testimonies was established in 1979: https://fortunoff.library.yale.edu/about-us/our-story/ [accessed 21 March 2024].

witness and an empathetic listener, turning traumatic memories into an acknowledged part of subjective reality (Laub 2009). Henry Greenspan with his psychological and dramaturgical background rather interpreted it as an ongoing process of exchanges between an eyewitness and an interviewer who go through joint phases of telling, reflecting and re-telling of Holocaust experiences and their aftermath (Greenspan et al. 2014, 204). At the same time, literary scholars began working on testimony. Lawrence Langer's work *Versions of Survival* (Langer 1982) and subsequent books became influential in interpreting Holocaust testimonies from outside of a strictly historical or psychological perspective. His trailblazing book, *Holocaust Testimonies: The Ruins of Memory* (Langer 1993), closely read testimonies in the Yale University Fortunoff Archive and sought to parse the differences between literary testimonies and audiovisual ones.

The 1990s saw a generational change with survivors who had been adolescents or younger adults in 1945 beginning to dominate discourses and draw public attention. Additionally, public awareness of Holocaust survivors' accounts further expanded, leading to the publication of new memoirs but also to the re-release of books that originally had been published in the 1940s, thus reaching new audiences. This increased awareness also spurred the beginning of a scholarly rediscovery of those early accounts and memoirs, initiating research into multiple testimonies as well as conscious efforts at re-interviewing survivors who had testified at previous points of their lives (Kangisser Cohen 2014, 69–71). The increasing international interest in survivor accounts led many survivors to return to their stories, interpreting and narrating them anew in the light of ageing and experience or adding material; however, the accompanying business appeal of survivor accounts also attracted a small number of impostors to write different stories of great individual suffering in the form of fictitious survivor accounts.[21]

Collection efforts of survivor accounts were taken to a new level—at least in quantitative terms—in the wake of Steven Spielberg's widely acclaimed box office hit *Schindler's List* (1993). While not replacing written texts, audiovisual testimonies became the preferred method of gathering as many survivor testimonies as possible and for recording the authentic voice and presence of the survivor for posterity. In the context of the rise of Oral History, recording testimony on video opened up new

---

[21] For a discussion of 'false' and 'embellished' testimony see Vice (2014) and the Epilogue to this book.

dimensions for understanding and analysing survivors' accounts in that it also documented facial expressions, physical reactions, bodily postures, etc., for researchers and audiences alike. The USC Shoah Foundation, created on the basis of the commercial success of the film, shaped interview guidelines that gave survivor accounts a fixed redemptive form. The structure moved from the pre-war, war and post-war personal experiences with a focus on persecution during the Holocaust, eventual survival, to a family-centred post-war life and a meaningful ending with lessons to be learned from a painful history. This was a departure from an earlier format, where many survivor accounts simply ended with liberation in 1945, towards an emphasis on the importance of peace, tolerance, reconciliation and the fight against antisemitism. While providing a welcome form of security and orientation for some, such an approach to a survivor account was seen as 'too controlling' by others who either just performed along to the expectations of the interviewer (Greenspan et al. 2014, 203) or even refused to follow the interviewer's lead. Lengyel's interview falls into the latter category as she consistently tried to establish her agenda and priorities in opposition to those of the interviewer.[22]

In the 2000s, collection efforts of survivor testimonies were redirected towards prioritising education and remembrance as the number of survivors still alive was dwindling and many were increasingly worried about leaving a lasting message of peace and reconciliation. Since then, research into testimonies has become more differentiated and comparative. This move includes studies that bring together the experiences of different incidents of genocide and extends to those that explore the variations introduced by the same person in different testimonies given over the course of their life (see, for example, Browning 2003; Matthäus 2009; Pollak et al. 2016). So far, scholars have mostly agreed that a diachronic analysis of a survivor's various testimonies shows, in the words of the late Dori Laub, 'an impressive narrative consistency' (Laub and Bodenstab 2010, 439) between and across those accounts. At the same time, experiences might be interpreted differently over time and, therefore, also be presented in a different way. Equally, changes in the biographical stages of survivors, their social role and self-understanding, all can result in distinct differences between biographical accounts over time (Schuch 2021, 333). And, of course, survivors also proactively use the opportunity

---

[22] For a discussion of the dynamic between Lengyel and her interviewer, Nancy Fisher, see Hannah Holtschneider's chapter.

of publicly speaking about their experiences to 'hone their accounts over many retellings' (Greenspan 2010b, 423). Public testimony is performative and impacts how memories and events are told (Kangisser Cohen 2014, 107). This shows that testimony can also be seen as a genre in its own right, with specific characteristics of form and content that challenge the idea of a single fixed definition of the term. Thus, Greenspan has argued that efforts by survivors to present their experiences in a way that makes them comprehensible to their listeners lay the basis for the specific format of a public testimony (Greenspan 2010a, 244).

Finally, ageing does not simply lead to a linear deterioration of memory, but can also enable survivors to master and assimilate their pasts better and find a more appropriate way to narrate those memories compared to previous stages of their lives (Greenspan et al. 2014, 212). Indeed, the perspective of age may allow survivors to talk more openly about memories that no longer cause traumatic pain.

In our collective research on Lengyel's testimonies we have been acutely aware that we never interviewed her ourselves, nor did we know her. Thus, many of the psychodynamic approaches espoused by scholars and practitioners like Greenspan and Laub are not entirely applicable to our engagement with Lengyel's testimonies. Lawrence Langer's work on different layers of memory and changes in relationship to the past in French non-Jewish Auschwitz survivor Charlotte Delbo's trilogy, *Auschwitz and After* (Delbo 2014), suggests ways of analysing testimonial statements of survivors that can no longer be engaged in dialogue. However, in the 2021 essay 'Memory and Invention in Lengyel's *Five Chimneys*' Langer claims that, 'many of the details of her [Lengyel's] account, though vivid and painful, range between the improbable and the impossible' (Langer 2021, 175). He proceeds to enumerate different ways in which Lengyel's testimonies, both written and audiovisual, cross, even for a Holocaust testimony, from fact into fiction. Langer himself says, at times, that his queries appear 'unseemly and even offensive', but he points out that a number of improbable events that Lengyel reports as factual make her text seem untrustworthy, and, thus, potentially open the door for discourses of denial that are based on inaccuracies in Holocaust testimonies. In the course of this volume, we will explore this challenge to Lengyel's veracity by Langer (Langer 2021), acknowledging that while anxiety about denialism is justified, denialists' theories are based on fantasy, conspiracy thinking and racism rather than evidence: open, honest and critical scholarship about testimony provides an antidote to denialism, rather than opening a door to it. His concerns about her testimonies will wend their way through several of our discussions and will be addressed directly in our Epilogue, as it had a significant impact on the direction of our collaboration.

We, therefore, find ourselves at an exciting crossroads where we must forge a new path towards understanding testimonies in the archives from the perspective of what Sheila E. Jelen has elsewhere called, 'viewer witnesses' (Jelen 2024, 38). In the absence of living testimonial performances, today's scholars of testimony must recognise their own responsibility to view texts and recordings—be they audio or audiovisual—as testimonial events in their own right, events that bring to their viewers and interlocutors a living presence. We become witnesses to the witnesses, 'participating in the testimonial experience as active interpreters, active catalysts in the performance, transmission and exigency of the testimony' (Jelen 2024, 51). Thus, challenges to the integrity of testimonies, be they historical, or biographical, take on new dimensions that require a certain kind of 'critical compassion' that may not have pertained in the presence of living survivors.[23] Like Laub, we are interested not necessarily in what Lengyel gets wrong, but in why she tells her story the ways she does and what that teaches us about Holocaust testimony (Felman and Laub 1992, 59–60); we are interested in ways of reading and understanding both in their own moments and as the discourse shifts over time.

Auschwitz and Birkenau from 1940/41 to 1945

Auschwitz concentration camp came into being on occupied Polish territory in a way similar to the installation of the early camps in the German Reich proper in 1933 (Dwork and Pelt 1996, 163–96). It served as an overflow camp because the regular prison system could not deal anymore with the massive influx of arrested members of Polish elites and the resistance in the aftermath of the German invasion (Rudorff 2018, 14–16). Because of the economic potential of the town of Oświęcim and its *hinterland*, it was annexed to the Reich proper although it was originally meant to be incorporated into the *General Government*, that is the non-annexed

---

[23] Relatedly, Dominick LaCapra coined the term 'empathic unsettlement', that is something that 'poses a barrier to closure in discourse and places in jeopardy harmonising or spiritually uplifting accounts of extreme events from which we attempt to derive reassurance or a benefit' (LaCapra 2014, 41–42).

Nazi-occupied Polish territory. The convenience of Oświęcim's operational railway tracks to the site contributed to the decision to erect a camp there. Before the camp was opened in June 1940 in former Polish army barracks (Auschwitz I), some thirty inmates of Sachsenhausen concentration camp were transferred there to serve as prisoner functionaries. At that time, the vast majority of the inmates were male.

At the same time, the economic development of the area was intensified. The SS started to cultivate large swaths of arable land for agriculture, while German industry—most notably IG Farben—started to build a huge facility to produce synthetic rubber close to the town of Monowice, roughly six kilometres from Oświęcim, where later a camp named Monowitz or Auschwitz III was built. This complex was intended to safeguard the German economy's independence from foreign imports. To have a sufficient supply of labour at hand for these purposes, a larger camp, originally meant especially for Soviet prisoners of war, was built in the autumn of 1941 near the town of Brzezinka, roughly three kilometres from Oświęcim, later named Birkenau or Auschwitz II (Fig. 1.2).

With the turn towards the indiscriminate killing of Jewish civilians in the wake of the German invasion of the Soviet Union in the summer of 1941, the systematic mass murder of the Jews of Europe began to unfold. The Nazi leadership and local SS and police authorities were looking for ways to murder large numbers of Jews, Roma and Sinti, various national resistance groups as well as a growing number of camp inmates who were either not fit, or no longer considered fit, for labour. Mass shootings outside of cities and villages as well as killings of smaller groups in gas vans were being carried out on a large scale. When *Operation Reinhardt*—the systematic murder of the Jews of occupied Poland—started in December 1941, Birkenau was redesigned to function as a killing site for Jews from the administrative district of Katowice as well as for Jews and Roma and Sinti from other parts of Europe.

In the wake of the Wannsee Conference of January 1942, the murder of the Jews of Europe under the auspices of the Reich Main Security Office began. Auschwitz-Birkenau became the centrepiece of this shocking state-sponsored crime with Jews from Central, Western, Southern and South-Eastern Europe forming the majority of the victims of mass deportations and gassing, after which their bodies were cremated and the ashes disposed. From the spring of 1942, arriving prisoners were separated by gender and 'selected' into groups destined for life or death based on perceived suitability for slave labour. This deadly routine was

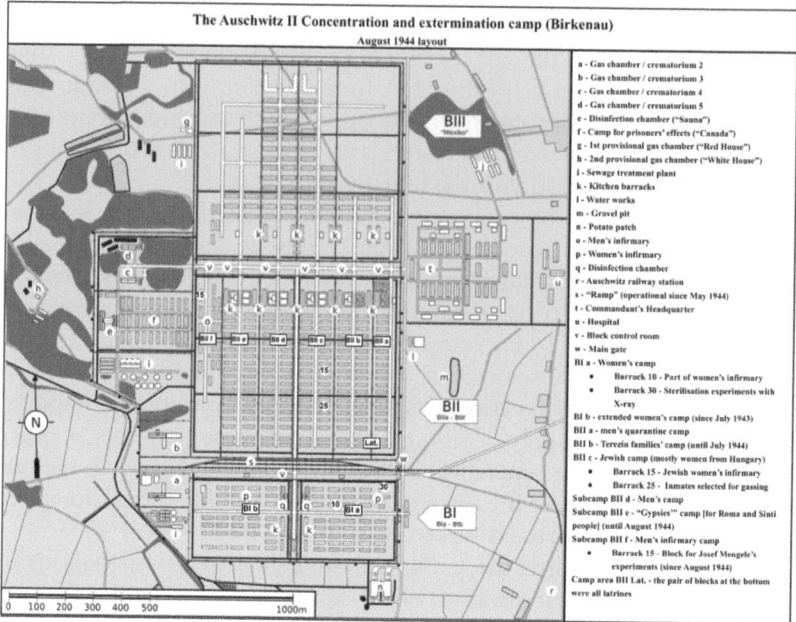

Fig. 1.2 Annotated map of Auschwitz-Birkenau in the summer of 1944 by HEROMAX: https://de.wikipedia.org/wiki/Datei:AUSCHWITZ-BIRKENAU. png (reproduced under a CC BY-SA licence found at https://creativecomm ons.org/licenses/by-sa/3.0/deed.en; the annotations were modified by Akiva Himelhoch to reflect the needs of this book)

often associated with camp doctors Josef Mengele and Fritz Klein. At the same time, prisoners selected for slave labour received their prisoner number as a tattoo on their forearm. Over the course of little more than one year, at first two improvised gas chambers and later four permanent killing facilities with gas chambers and ovens for cremation were installed at Birkenau. Until the turn of the year 1942/43, pregnant women were killed at Birkenau immediately after selection. Afterwards, the lives of the mothers were spared in order to use them as forced labourers while the babies were killed. This went on until the suspension of killings by gas in November 1944. Only non-Jewish babies had a chance of survival once they were regularly registered as prisoners beginning in June 1943 (Rudorff 2020, 91).

Apart from those deportees who were killed upon arrival and those who were forced to labour under appalling and often life-threatening circumstances, there were also some who were selected for medical experiments. From autumn 1942 onwards, Auschwitz I and Birkenau became a 'centre for medical research' (Rudorff 2018, 16:34–35). Doctors carried out gruesome and cruel experiments to sterilise their victims or to try out newly developed medication, for example, to treat typhus. Josef Mengele became the most notorious of the doctors, mostly because of his choice of twins, dwarfs, pregnant women and newborn babies for scientific studies which cost the lives of most of them and made him a regular at the selections of newly arrived deportees to identify fresh victims for his research.

Mengele had been working in Auschwitz-Birkenau since 30 May 1943. He was initially the head camp doctor in the so-called 'Gypsy camp', which was located in camp section B II e, and after its dissolution at the beginning of August 1944, he relocated his research laboratory to the prisoner infirmary camp B II f and succeeded Fritz Klein as camp doctor for the women's camp (Zofka 1986, 255). Therefore, the infirmary in B II c, where Olga Lengyel was forced to work, came under his responsibility, as well.

The majority of the genocide by gassing took place from the spring of 1942 until the autumn of 1943. However, after Germany invaded Hungary in March 1944, the mass murder of Jews living under Hungarian rule became the single deadliest part of the entire genocidal operation (Longerich 2010, 407; Braham and Kovács 2016). With a view to the huge operational task of the mass murder of Jews from Greater Hungary, the SS conducted a leadership shake-up at Auschwitz that brought previous camp commandant Rudolf Höß, who had been there from May 1940 to November 1943, back as garrison commander of the entire camp complex and newly introduced Josef Kramer, previously commandant of the Natzweiler-Struthof concentration camp, as commandant of Birkenau.

In May 1944, Lengyel and her immediate family members were deported to Auschwitz-Birkenau; she was the only member of her family to survive. Soon after her arrival, Lengyel was assigned to work in the inmates' sick bay of camp section B II c, due to her professional background as a surgical nurse. This camp infirmary for Jewish women was established in July 1944, presumably in Barrack 15, and became the workplace for Lengyel and her fellow inmate Dr. Gisella Perl (Rudorff 2018,

16–19), initially under the command of SS camp doctor Fritz Klein. Sheila E. Jelen explores the relationship between Perl's and Lengyel's testimonies in her chapter.

In January 1945, there were still about 67,000 inmates in the entire Auschwitz camp complex. Between 17 and 21 January 1945, around 56,000 prisoners, among them Olga Lengyel, were put on so-called evacuation marches (also known as 'death marches') towards concentration camps within Germany proper (Rudorff 2018, 75–76). As they received neither adequate food rations nor suitable clothing, around 15,000 prisoners died along the roads and rail tracks, either directly killed by SS guards or perishing from the disastrous circumstances.

Trials of Nazi Crimes

Lengyel never testified in court about the crimes committed at Auschwitz. She did testify, though, on 28 January 1972 in the long-running pre-trial investigation against Josef Mengele by the Frankfurt/Main public prosecutor's office (Völklein 1999). However, as Mengele was never brought to trial, this remained without legal consequences. In the immediate postwar period, she closely followed the initial steps of the victorious powers to bring Nazi perpetrators and their auxiliaries to justice. In the English version of her book, she wrote about her impressions of the first British Bergen-Belsen trial (17 September to 17 November 1945) which proved influential for the ways she referred to a number of prominent perpetrators (Lengyel 2000, 24, 153, 162). At the same time, we can only speculate how much of an interest she—herself having been a prisoner functionary—took in the fact that among the forty-five defendants in this trial, there were also twelve former prisoner functionaries. Given her own medical background as a surgical nurse and her enforced work in the prisoner infirmary in Birkenau, we may also at least assume that she would have paid attention to the first two of the Nuremberg Military Tribunals which had medical experiments on human beings and other crimes committed by doctors in numerous concentration camps high on their agendas.[24] There is no documented evidence that Lengyel herself tried to make any personal contribution to those trials, but in general,

---

[24] The Doctors' Trial (1st) took place 9 December 1946–20 August 1947 and the Milch Trial (2nd) 2 January–14 April 1947.

she seemed to be in favour of the ways perpetrators had been dealt with by post-war judiciaries (Lengyel 2000, 228).

Lengyel's own articulations, in her testimonies, about her role as a medical functionary at the camps, working closely under the direction of Fritz Klein become better understood when read within the context of the post-war trials focused on medical personnel. Indeed, in her written testimony, she identifies moments where she was ordered to perpetrate violent crimes against other innocent victims; there she describes her own forced implication in the murder of a group of young children whom she was instructed to freeze to death through repeated bathing and exposure, in order to spare the bullets necessary for their execution. Even as she describes her own role in their deaths, Lengyel dedicates her memoir to the memory of those children (Lengyel 2000, 225–27). The murky line between being a victim and being a perpetrator—what Primo Levi has famously described as 'the grey zone'—was fully on display in the post-war trials. Lengyel's presentation of her own participation in the medical culture at Auschwitz may be, to some extent, a personal defence, as well as a defence of even extreme cases of doctors such as the Transylvanian-German SS doctor Fritz Klein, with whom she claimed an acquaintance based on shared cultural background.

In the British military trial at Lüneburg on the crimes committed in the Bergen-Belsen concentration camp which lay in its zone of occupation,[25] for the first time, the legal concept of a 'Common Design' (although back then still referred to as 'Conspiracy') was prosecuted as a statutory offence in connection with Nazi crimes: the operation of a concentration camp was already considered a crime, so that willingly and knowingly participating in that operation could be considered criminal. Christoph Thonfeld discusses this in more detail in his chapter. Thereby, British military justice established a point of reference for its future use to deal with Nazi crimes. The trial was conducted in accordance with British military criminal law and the defendants were charged exclusively for war crimes. Crimes committed in the Auschwitz concentration camp complex were tried there as well, because many of the defendants had been stationed in Auschwitz, Birkenau or Monowitz before their transfer

---

[25] On the Bergen-Belsen Trial, see Bergen-Belsen, 2006–2015, http://www.bergenbelsen.co.uk/pages/Trial/TrialFront/TrialFront_01.html (accessed 3 March 2024).

to Bergen-Belsen. Among the seventeen SS men and sixteen female supervisors who were tried, Birkenau commandant Josef Kramer, camp doctor Fritz Klein and wardress Irma Grese were all sentenced to death and eventually executed in Hamelin in 1946. Twelve former prisoner functionaries were also among the accused. Eight received prison terms between five years and life, while four were acquitted, showing the broad range of punishments that were handed out to former prisoner functionaries.

The Doctors' Trial is of particular relevance to Lengyel, too, who by her own account worked as a medical prisoner functionary in the Jewish women's infirmary at Birkenau. Held from December 1946 to August 1947, this was the first of the US Nuremberg Military Tribunals. Criminal proceedings were conducted against twenty-three high-ranking German physicians and medicine-related administrators, charged with participation in war crimes and crimes against humanity. Josef Mengele was not among them, as he was still at large at that time. The trial highlighted the strong presence of the medical profession in the SS, its numerous connections with the *Wehrmacht* (German army)—especially the air force—and also saw the indictment of one female camp doctor in Herta Oberheuser, who had been responsible for the medical mistreatment of inmates at Ravensbrück concentration camp. While the mass murder of disabled and mentally ill people played a major role in the trial, human experiments also formed an essential part. The trial was not only momentous in bringing members of a highly respected functional elite to justice but it also served as a forum for the victims to give voice to the suffering inflicted on them and its consequences (Ebbinghaus and Roth 2007, 127). Medical experiments at Buchenwald, Dachau, Natzweiler, Ravensbrück and Sachsenhausen concentration camps—with former inmates from Auschwitz also among the victims—were on the prosecution's agenda.

On the whole, Holocaust survivors' perception of the International Military Tribunal and its follow-up trials was clearly ambivalent. While they actively welcomed the efforts that were made by the Allies to bring perpetrators to justice, there was disappointment over the fact that the genocide of the Jews factually played only a supporting role in the trials. Only a few survivors were called up to the witness stand at Nuremberg to testify against their former tormentors (Jockusch 2012, 667). There was also dissatisfaction with the way the survivors who were called upon as witnesses were treated while giving evidence. Mostly the defence counsels, but also prosecutors, expected them to provide exact dates, times and accompanying circumstances when testifying about the crimes of the defendants. Given the situation in extermination camps and concentration camps, hardly any of them could provide these to a degree that would have been deemed satisfactory in the courtroom (Lasker-Wallfisch 2014, 310).

Gender

Lengyel's testimonies have been read, from their first appearance in 1946, as an invaluable contribution to the documentation of women's experiences in the war. This is not only due to the fact that Lengyel was a woman and mother who was sent to Auschwitz and wrote about her experiences there, but also because she represented, in her writing, the Jewish women's infirmary at Birkenau, with a special emphasis on the persecution of pregnant women and their infants. One would think that understanding women's experiences in the Holocaust as separate from men's would be self-evident. However, that has not been the case. For our analyses of Lengyel's testimonies, we present an overview of gendered approaches to the Holocaust, both generally, but also as they specifically pertain to readings of Lengyel.

Although the earliest attempts at documentation of Holocaust history, made by Emanuel Ringelblum in the Warsaw Ghetto, acknowledged the necessity of a separate and focused study of the experiences of women, systematic accounts of the unique experiences of women during the war were quite belated (Ringelblum 2015). This can be attributed to a number of different factors: first, women's experiences of sexual exploitation, rape, abortion, pregnancy, infanticide and the death of children were considered too sensitive for discussion in many testimonies, both from the perspective of the survivor, but also from the perspective of researchers.[26] Second, the Holocaust was considered by many to be an attack on all Jews and not on any particular segment within that population. For many years, to focus separately on the experiences of women as different from those of men in the Holocaust was considered an inappropriate application of a feminist lens to discussions of genocide. Indeed, with the publication of Dalia Ofer's and Lenore Weizman's edited volume, *Women*

---

[26] Still in 2011, Christopher Browning writes that in interviews with him, women were reluctant to discuss with him 'childbirth, infanticide, abortion, sex, and rape [...] Nor were they topics that I felt comfortable broaching in interviews, particularly with female survivors many years my senior' (Browning 2011, 185).

in the Holocaust (Ofer and Weitzman 1998), a public debate broke out on the pages of *Commentary* magazine when Hillel Halkin and Gabriel Schoenfeld responded to the volume by excoriating scholars whom they perceived to be exploiting the study of the Holocaust 'in the name of a naked ideological agenda' (Schoenfeld 1998; see also Halkin 1998; see also Jelen's chapter in this volume).

In the first book length study of women in the Holocaust, titled *Women Surviving the Holocaust* (Katz and Ringelheim 1983) which was constituted by the proceedings of a conference that took place at Stern College in New York that same year, Joan Ringelheim and Esther Katz, the conference's organisers and the book's editors, made a case for pursuing a gendered analysis of the Holocaust on two tracks: to recover the experiences of women and in so doing, to 'nuance our understanding of Holocaust history'.[27] As argued by subsequent scholars who, in the last several decades, have addressed the repressed and ignored experiences of women in the Holocaust, it is critical to identify and analyse women's narratives both on an individual and a collective level.[28]

Lengyel's *Five Chimneys*, published just after the war, and focused in large part on the role of sexual bartering at Auschwitz as well as the experience of pregnancy, childbirth and infanticide there, has been featured in various studies pertaining specifically to the experience of women in the camps.[29] The attack on 'Jewish wombs' and the 'gynecological genocide' that unfolded during the Holocaust as the result of the Nazi perception of the Jewish female body as the site of Jewish continuity, finds expression in Lengyel's testimonies (Finley-Croswhite 2021, 103). Her work has been featured in studies of women's Holocaust testimonies by authors such as Petra Schweitzer, Carmelle Stephens and Edit Jeges, with an emphasis on the marginalisation of women's narratives within mainstream Holocaust history (Schweitzer 2016; Stephens 2020; Jeges 2015).

---

[27] Joan Ringelheim outlines the birth of the discourse of gender and the Holocaust in her essay: 'Women and the Holocaust: A Reconsideration of Research' (Ringelheim 1985). See also Katz and Ringelheim (1983).

[28] In addition to the authors and texts in Ringelheim and Katz, see also Baer and Goldenberg (2003), Rittner and Roth (1993), Hardman (2000), Waxman (2017).

[29] On the concept of 'sexual barter', see Hájková (2013), Cushman (2020). For an exploration of Lengyel's *Five Chimneys* and 'sexual exchange' see Bos (2024). Indeed, the most recent issue of *The Journal of Holocaust Research* is dedicated to 'Gender-based and sexual violence in the Holocaust': Glowacka and Mühlhäuser (2024).

While aspects of Lengyel's testimonies have been contested, in this volume Sheila E. Jelen argues that Lengyel's unique representation of the experiences of the women who worked in the Jewish women's infirmary in Auschwitz-Birkenau provides a valuable reflection of the collective experience of women in the camps. In her essay on women medical practitioners during the Holocaust and their acts of resistance because of their privileged position as recognised experts and leaders in their community, Noa Gidron cites Dr. Margita Schwalbová (1915–2002) as saying that 'the center of the resistance movement, which in 1943 became an international movement, was inside the hospital' (Gidron 2020, 46). While Schwalbová was forced to work as a prisoner doctor in Auschwitz I (Barrack 10), a context different from Lengyel's in Birkenau's Jewish women's infirmary, her observation serves as a reference point for thinking about the nature of resistance. Indeed, Lengyel claims to have been involved in the resistance as a member of the Birkenau female medical corps (located mainly in B I a, while the Jewish women's infirmary was located in B II c), but because she has not been mentioned by any of the historical accounts, her participation in the underground has been called into question.[30] Resistance, however, necessarily extends far beyond armed battle. While Lengyel states that she was involved in carrying explosives between members of the resistance, perhaps she tells this story because she feels that resistance can only be presented, in post-war France, in the idiom of those from the armed French underground who were deported to Auschwitz. The resistance she describes more eloquently, and more valuably, however, can be found in her account of the comportment of the female medical staff in the Birkenau Jewish women's infirmary who fought to save mothers by disposing of their infants, or who admitted as patients those who were destined to be chosen for the gas in the next selection, sparing them the selection and their immediate deaths.

The need to reclaim women's narratives of the Holocaust, to redefine resistance within the context of the Nazi Holocaust, is embedded in the testimonies of Olga Lengyel. Just as she might have elaborated the nature of the resistance activities in which she engaged so they more closely resembled what was conventionally figured as resistance after the

---

[30] In private conversations, Gabriel Finder, an expert in the resistance at Auschwitz, asserted his scepticism over Lengyel's participation because he did not see her mentioned in the literature.

war, so too might she have exaggerated her role in the Jewish women's infirmary at Birkenau.

The silences surrounding women's unique Holocaust experiences in Holocaust discourse, even to this day, become articulated in the very questions that have been raised about the veracity of Lengyel's testimonies. Nevertheless, Lengyel taps into experiences that must be told, even if she did not experience them herself, as a way to voice the silences imposed upon women and on women's experiences in Holocaust discourse.

What to Expect from the Chapters that Follow

This book is designed to illustrate the insights that can be gained from a multidisciplinary approach to a single survivor's testimonies. Of the four contributors to this volume, two are historians, one is a literary scholar, and one is a translation expert, though these disciplinary labels do not do justice to our cross-cutting interests and shared understandings. Peter Davies considers the effects of translation on the writing, publication and reception of testimony. His contribution to this volume explores the publication and translation history of Lengyel's written testimony, asking questions about the shifts between the French and English versions of the text. Sheila E. Jelen focuses on the sustained literary narratives represented by Holocaust testimonies, both oral and written, and reads Lengyel within the context of gender studies and in dialogue with other texts by female survivors of the Birkenau Jewish women's infirmary. Hannah Holtschneider works on ego documents and private archives in the writing of history. Her chapter explores articulations of personal agency within the 'ecologies of witnessing' (Pollin-Galay 2019), conditioned by historical context and audience expectations, in which Lengyel's testimonies developed. Christoph Thonfeld integrates the study of multiple testimonies of survivors with perpetrator research. He explores the role of the representation of perpetrators in Lengyel's accounts and how the early public perception of Nazi perpetrators was shaped by both survivors' testimonies and media coverage.

All our chapters consider ideas of agency in relation to Lengyel's testimony, as expressed in a variety of different ways: the multiple iterations of her story in the late 1940s that offer parallel but slightly different accounts in French and English, the differences between editions, the spectre of a Hungarian text or at least some passages first formulated in

Hungarian, the role of translation and translators, of editors and the lack of actual editing and fact-checking, of publishing houses, of economic considerations and of ideas about audience. We bring these together with analyses of Lengyel's narrative strategy that emphasises particular perceptions of gender roles, sexuality, morality, motherhood and infanticide. We also consider self-presentation alongside Lengyel's giving evidence of crimes to a wider public and in relation to perpetrators and war crimes trials.

We have all worked intensively with survivor testimony from different perspectives and we read and listen to Lengyel's words with different questions in mind: the moments of overlap but also of difference between our readings are what have made our collaboration fruitful. We have written this Introduction together and have each taken on a single chapter reflecting our own concerns and ways of reading. Despite the individual names above each chapter, the process has been collaborative, characterised by dialogue and disagreement. We have never tried to force ourselves to agree or to achieve any form of synthesis; instead, we began with a shared set of testimony texts and a range of established scholarly responses to them, discussing and debating the questions that arose from our joint reading practices. We started from within what we assumed were shared approaches to testimony and found that our perspectives on the texts were rooted in specific disciplinary contexts and traditions. The discovery of our different reading practices is what drives this project forwards. The common ground we share is, therefore, not our goal but has been our point of departure.

References

Baer, Elizabeth Roberts, and Myrna Goldenberg, eds. 2003. *Experience and Expression: Women, the Nazis, and the Holocaust*. Detroit: Wayne State University Press.

Bloch, Claudette. 1946. *Témoignages Sur Auschwitz*. Paris: Edition de l'Amicale des déportés d'Auschwitz.

Bos, Pascale R. 2024. Barter, Prostitution, Abuse? Reframing Experiences of Sexual Exchange during the Holocaust. *The Journal of Holocaust Research*. https://doi.org/10.1080/25785648.2024.2383037.

Braham, Randolph L. 1998. The Holocaust in Hungary: A Retrospective Analysis. In *The Nazis' Last Victims: The Holocaust in Hungary*, ed. Randolph L. Braham and Scott Miller, 27–43. Detroit: Wayne State University Press.

Braham, Randolph L., and András Kovács, eds. 2016. *The Holocaust in Hungary: Seventy Years Later*. Budapest, Hungary: Central European University, Jewish Studies Program.

Braham, Randolph L., and Scott Miller, eds. 1998. *The Nazis' Last Victims: The Holocaust in Hungary*. Detroit: Wayne State University Press.

Browning, Christopher R. 2003. *Collected Memories: Holocaust History and Postwar Testimony*. George L. Mosse Series in Modern European Cultural and Intellectual History. Madison: The University of Wisconsin Press.

Browning, Christopher R. 2011. *Remembering Survival: Inside a Nazi Slave-Labor Camp*. 1. publ. as a paperback. New York, NY: Norton.

Carmilly-Weinberger, Moshe. 1994. *The Road to Life: The Rescue Operation of Jewish Refugees on the Hungarian-Romanian Border in Transylvania, 1936–1944*. New York: Shengold.

Case, Holly. 2007. 'Navigating Identities: The Jews of Kolozsvár (Cluj) and the Hungarian Administration 1940–1944'. In *Osteuropa Vom Weltkrieg Zur Wende*, edited by Wolfgang Mueller and Michael Portmann, 39–53. Verlag der Österreichischen Akademie der Wissenschaften. https://doi.org/10.1553/0x0013e345.

Cushman, Sarah M. 2020. 'Sexuality, Sexual Violence, and Sexual Barter in the Auschwitz-Birkenau Women's Camp'. In *Agency and the Holocaust: Essays in Honor of Debórah Dwork*, edited by Thomas Kühne and Mary Jane Rein, 105–21. Cham: Springer International Publishing. https://doi.org/10.1007/978-3-030-38998-7_7.

D'Arcy, David. 2015. 'Holocaust Survivor's Art Last Seen in Cuba', 22 December 2015. https://www.theartnewspaper.com/2015/12/22/holoca ust-survivors-art-last-seen-in-cuba.

Delbo, Charlotte. 2014. *Auschwitz and After*. Translated by Rosette C. Lamont. 2nd edition. New Haven, Connecticut: Yale University Press.

Doßmann, Axel. 2022. 'Überforderte Zeugenschaft. Holocaust-Interviews in der Geschichtskultur und historischen Bildung'. In *Jenseits der Erinnerung - Verbrechensgeschichte begreifen: Impulse für die kritische Auseinandersetzung mit dem Nationalsozialismus nach dem Ende der Zeitgenossenschaft*, edited by Volkhard Knigge and Ulrike Löffler, 234–58. Buchenwald und Mittelbau-Dora - Forschungen und Reflexionen, Band 4. Göttingen: Wallstein Verlag.

Dwork, Debórah, and R.J. van Pelt. 1996. *Auschwitz, 1270 to the Present*, 1st ed. New York: W.W., Norton & Company.

Ebbinghaus, Angelika, and Karl-Heinz Roth. 2007. 'Medizinverbrechen vor Gericht'. In *Dachauer Prozesse: NS-Verbrechen vor amerikanischen Militärgerichten in Dachau 1945 - 48; Verfahren, Ergebnisse, Nachwirkungen*, edited by Ludwig Eiber, 2. Aufl, 126–59. Dachauer Symposien zur Zeitgeschichte 7. Göttingen: Wallstein.

Eisen, George. 2023. *A Summer of Mass Murder: 1941 Rehearsal for the Hungarian Holocaust*. West Lafayette, Indiana: Purdue University Press.

Emmanuel, Pierre. 1945. Hymne Pour Le Retour Des Captifs. *Poésie* 45 (26–27): 41–48.

Felman, Shoshana, and Dori Laub. 1992. *Testimony: Crises of Witnessing in Literature, Psychoanalysis, and History*. New York, NY: Routledge.

Finley-Croswhite, Annette. 2021. Un(B)Earable: Pregnant Bodies and Obstetrical Genocide. In *Recognizing the Past in the Present: New Studies on Medicine before, During, and After the Holocaust*, ed. Sabine Hildebrandt, Miriam Offer, and Michael A. Grodin, 103–124. New York: Berghahn Books.

Gidron, Noam. 2020. 'Jewish Women Medical Practitioners Who Rescued Fellow Jews during the Holocaust'. *Nashim: A Journal of Jewish Women's Studies & Gender Issues*, no. 36, 39. https://doi.org/10.2979/nashim.36.1.04.

Glowacka, Dorota, and Regina Mühlhäuser. 2024. Gender-Based and Sexual Violence in the Holocaust: On the Importance of Writing This History Today. *The Journal of Holocaust Research*. https://doi.org/10.1080/257 85648.2024.2370632.

Greenspan, Henry. 2000. 'The Awakening of Memory Survivor Testimony in the First Years after the Holocaust, and Today'. Monna and Otto Weinman Lecture Series. United States Holocaust Memorial Museum.

Greenspan, Henry. 2010a. *On Listening to Holocaust Survivors: Beyond Testimony*, 2nd ed. St. Paul, Minnesota: Paragon House.

Greenspan, Henry. 2010b. Survivors' Accounts. *Oxford University Press*. https://doi.org/10.1093/oxfordhb/9780199211869.003.0028.

Greenspan, Henry. 2015 'From Testimony to Recounting: Reflections from Forty Years of Listening to Holocaust Survivors'. In *Beyond Testimony and Trauma*, edited by Steven High, 141–69. University of British Columbia Press. https://doi.org/10.59962/9780774828949-007.

Greenspan, Henry, Sara R. Horowitz, Éva Kovács, Berel Lang, Dori Laub, Kenneth Waltzer, and Annette Wieviorka. 2014. 'Engaging Survivors: Assessing "Testimony" and "Trauma" as Foundational Concepts'. *Dapim: Studies on the Holocaust* 28 (3): 190–226. https://doi.org/10.1080/232 56249.2014.951909.

Hájková, Anna. 2013. 'Sexual Barter in Times of Genocide: Negotiating the Sexual Economy of the Theresienstadt Ghetto'. *Signs: Journal of Women in Culture and Society* 38 (3): 503–33. https://doi.org/10.1086/668607.

Halkin, Hillel. 1998. 'Feminizing Jewish Studies'. *Commentary*, February. https://www.commentary.org/articles/hillel-halkin/feminizing-jewish-stu dies/.

Hand, Seán., and Steven T. Katz, eds. 2015. *Post-Holocaust France and the Jews, 1945–1955*. Elie Wiesel Center for Judaic Studies Series. New York: New York University Press.

Hardman, Anna. 2000. *Women and the Holocaust*. London: Holocaust Educational Trust.

Jeges, Edit. 2015. 'Gendering the Cultural Memory of the Holocaust: A Comparative Analysis of a Memoir and a Video Testimony by Olga Lengyel'. In *Women and the Holocaust*, edited by Andrea Pető, Louise Hecht, and Karolina Krasuska, 233–53. Central European University Press. http://www.jstor.org/stable/https://doi.org/10.7829/j.ctt1t6p69c.

Jelen, Sheila E. 2024. *Testimonial Montage: A Family of Israeli Holocaust Testimonies from the Cracow Ghetto Resistance*. Lanham: Lexington Books.

Jockusch, Laura. 2012. *Collect and Record! Jewish Holocaust Documentation in Early Postwar Europe*. Oxford: Oxford University Press.

Kangisser Cohen, Sharon. 2014. *Testimony and Time: Holocaust Survivors Remember*. Jerusalem: Yad Vashem, the International institute for Holocaust research, the Diana Zborowski center for the study of the aftermath of the Holocaust.

Katz, Esther, and Joan Ringelheim, eds. 1983. *Proceedings of the Conference on Women Surviving—the Holocaust*. Occasional Papers from the Institute for Research in History. New York, NY Institute for Research in History.

LaCapra, Dominick. 2014. *Writing History, Writing Trauma: With a New Preface*. Parallax: Re-Visions of Culture and Society. Baltimore: Johns Hopkins University Press.

Langbein, Hermann. 1972. *Menschen in Auschwitz*. 1. unveränderter Nachdruck. Frankfurt am Main: FISCHER Taschenbuch.

Langbein, Hermann, and Harry Zohn. 2004. *People in Auschwitz*. Chapel Hill: The University of North Carolina Press.

Langer, Lawrence. 1982. *Versions of Survival: The Holocaust and the Human Spirit*. SUNY Series in Modern Jewish Literature and Culture. Albany: State Univ. of New York Pr.

Langer, Lawrence. 1993. *Holocaust Testimonies: The Ruins of Memory*. New Haven: Yale University Press.

Langer, Lawrence. 2021. 'Memory and Invention in Olga Lengyel's Five Chimneys'. In *The Afterdeath of the Holocaust*, 169–95. Cham: Springer International Publishing.

Lasker-Wallfisch, Anita. 2014. *Ihr sollt die Wahrheit erben: die Cellistin von Auschwitz; Erinnerungen*. 2. Aufl., Ungekürzte Ausg. rororo Großdruck 33251. Reinbek bei Hamburg: Rowohlt Taschenbuch Verl.

Laub, Dori. 2009. On Holocaust Testimony and Its "Reception" within Its Own Frame, as a Process in Its Own Right: A Response to "Between History and Psychoanalysis" by Thomas Trezise. *History and Memory* 21 (1): 127. https://doi.org/10.2979/his.2009.21.1.127.

Laub, Dori, and Johanna Bodenstab. 2010. 'Twenty-Five Years Later: Revisiting Testimonies of Holocaust Survivors'. In *Hitler's Slaves: Life Stories of Forced Labourers in Nazi-Occupied Europe*, edited by Alexander von Plato, Almut Leh, and Christoph Thonfeld, 1st ed, 426–40. New York: Berghahn Books.

Le Quotidien de l'art. 2015. 'À La Recherche de La Collection d'Olga Lengyel à Cuba', 23 December 2015. https://www.lequotidiendelart.com/articles/8446-%C3%A0-la-recherche-de-la-collection-d-olga-lengyel-%C3%A0-cuba.html.

Lengyel, Olga. 1946. *Souvenirs de l'au-delà*. Translated by Ladislas Gara. Paris: Éditions du Bateau Ivre.

Lengyel, Olga. 1947a. *Five Chimneys: The Story of Auschwitz*. Translated by Clifford Coch and Paul P. Weiss. Chicago: Ziff Davis Publishing Co.

Lengyel, Olga. 1947b. *I Survived Hitler's Ovens*. Chicago: Ziff Davis Publishing Co.

Lengyel, Olga. 1957. *I Survived Hitler's Ovens*. New York: Avon.

Lengyel, Olga. 1959. 'Camp of Captive Women'. *For Men Only* 6 (11): 12–15, 54.

Lengyel, Olga. 2000. *Five Chimneys: A Woman Survivor's True Story of Auschwitz*. Chicago, IL: Academy Chicago Publ.

Lengyel, Olga, and Ágnes Stier. 2021. *Öt kémény: egy auschwitzi túlélő igaz története*. Szeged: Lazi Könyvkiadó.

Longerich, Peter. 2010. *Holocaust: The Nazi Persecution and Murder of the Jews*. Oxford: Oxford University Press.

Matthäus, Jürgen., ed. 2009. *Approaching an Auschwitz Survivor: Holocaust Testimony and Its Transformations*. New York, NY: Oxford University Press. https://doi.org/10.1093/acprof:oso/9780195389159.001.0001.

McNeish, James. 2007. *The Sixth Man: The Extraordinary Life of Paddy Costello*. Auckland: Random House New Zealand.

Mendelsohn, Ezra. 2001. *The Jews of East Central Europe between the World Wars*. Nachdr. A Midland Book 418. Bloomington, Ind: Indiana Univ. Press.

Ofer, Dalia, and Lenore J. Weitzman, eds. 1998. *Women in the Holocaust*. New Haven, Conn.: Yale Univ. Press.

Patai, Raphael. 2015. *The Jews of Hungary: History, Culture, Psychology*. Detroit: Wayne State University Press.

von Plato, Alexander, Almut Leh, and Christoph Thonfeld, eds. 2010. *Hitler's Slaves: Life Stories of Forced Labourers in Nazi-Occupied Europe*, 1st ed. New York: Berghahn Books.

Pollak, Michael, Christian Fleck, Gerhard Botz, and Matthias Pollak. 2016. *Die Grenzen des Sagbaren: Lebensgeschichten von KZ-Überlebenden als Augenzeugenberichte und als Identitätsarbeit*. 2. Auflage. Wiener Studien zur Zeitgeschichte, Band 1. Wien Münster: Lit.

Pollin-Galay, Hannah. 2019. *Ecologies of Witnessing: Language, Place, and Holocaust Testimony*. New Haven: Yale University Press.

Ringelblum, Emmanuel. 2015. *Notes From the Warsaw Ghetto*. San Francisco: Normanby Press.

Ringelheim, Joan. 1985. Women and the Holocaust: A Reconsideration of Research. *Signs* 10 (4): 741–761.

Rittner, Carol, and John K. Roth, eds. 1993. *Different Voices: Women and the Holocaust*, 1st ed. St. Paul, Minn: Paragon House.

Rudorff, Andrea, ed. 2018. *Das KZ Auschwitz 1942–1945 Und Die Zeit Der Todesmärsche 1944/45*. Vol. 16. Die Verfolgung und Ermordung der Europäischen Juden durch das Nationalsozialistische Deutschland 1933–1945. De Gruyter. https://doi.org/10.1515/9783110573787.

Rudorff, Andrea, ed. 2020. 'Einführung in die deutsche Ausgabe'. In *Ich war eine Ärztin in Auschwitz*, by Gisella Perl, 6–36. Wiesbaden: Marix Verlag.

Schoenfeld, Gabriel. 1998. 'Auschwitz and the Professors'. *Commentary*, June. https://www.commentary.org/articles/gabriel-schoenfeld/auschwitz-and-the-professors/.

Schpun, Mônica Raisa. 2010. L'Immigration Juive Dans La France de l'après-Guerre, 1945–1950. In *Terre d'exil, Terre d'asile: Migrations Juives En France Aux XIXe et XXe Siècles*, ed. Colette Zytnicki, 115–131. Paris: Éditions de l'éclat.

Schuch, Daniel. 2021. *Transformationen Der Zeugenschaft: Von David P. Boders Frühen Audiointerviews Zur Wiederbefragung Als Holocaust Testimony*. Buchenwald Und Mittelbau-Dora-- Forschungen Und Reflexionen, Band 1. Göttingen: Wallstein Verlag.

Schweitzer, Petra M. 2016. *Gendered Testimonies of the Holocaust: Writing Life*. Lanham, Maryland: Lexington Books.

Stephens, Carmelle. 2020. Saints and Martyrs: Popular Maternal Tropes in Holocaust Memoir. *The Journal of Holocaust Research* 34 (2): 95–110. https://doi.org/10.1080/25785648.2020.1741847.

Styron, William. 1997. A Wheel of Evil Come Full Circle: The Making of "Sophie's Choice." *The Sewanee Review* 105 (3): 395–400.

Styron, William. 2010. *Sophie's Choice*. New York, NY: Open Road Integrated Media.

Tibori Szabó, Zoltán. 2016. 'The Holocaust in Transylvania'. In *The Holocaust in Hungary: Seventy Years Later*, edited by Randolph L. Braham and András Kovács, 147–82. Budapest, Hungary: Central European University, Jewish Studies Program.

Turda, Marius. 2016. Redemptive Family Narratives: Olga Lengyel and the Textuality of the Holocaust. *Archiva Moldaviae* 8: 69–82.

Vice, Sue. 2014. 'False and Embellished Holocaust Testimony'. In *Textual Deceptions: False Memoirs and Literary Hoaxes in the Contemporary Era*, by Sue Vice, 142–202. Edinburgh University Press. https://doi.org/10.3366/edinburgh/9780748675555.001.0001.

Völklein, Ulrich. 1999. *Josef Mengele: Der Arzt von Auschwitz*. 1. Aufl. Göttingen: Steidl.

Waxman, Zoë. 2017. Women in the Holocaust: A Feminist History. *Oxford University Press*. https://doi.org/10.1093/acprof:oso/9780199608683.001.0001.

Weigel, Sigrid. 2023. Bearing Witness as a Boundary Case: Survivor Testimony, Legal Testimony and Historical Testimony. In *The Palgrave Handbook of Testimony and Culture*, ed. Sara Jones and Roger Woods, 39–63. Cham: Springer International Publishing. https://doi.org/10.1007/978-3-031-13794-5_3.

Wieviorka, Annette. 2006. *The Era of the Witness*. Translated by Jared Stark. Ithaca, N.Y. London: Cornell University Press.

Wormser, Olga, and Henri Michel. 1955. *Tragédie de La Déportation 1940–1945. (9. Mille)*. Paris: Hachette.

Zofka, Zdenek. 1986. Der KZ-Arzt Josef Mengele Zur Typologie Eines NS-Verbrechers. *Vierteljahrshefte Für Zeitgeschichte* 34 (2): 245–267.

WEBSITES (LAST ACCESSED MARCH 2024)

'Voices of the Holocaust' (Illinois Institute of Technology, 2009/2021), https://voices.library.iit.edu/

http://www.bergenbelsen.co.uk/pages/Trial/TrialFront/TrialFront_01.html

https://fortunoff.library.yale.edu/about-us/our-story/

https://www.justice.gov/sites/default/files/fcsc/pages/attachments/2014/12/18/cuban_basic_claimant_info_value.pdf

https://www.toli.us/

Olga Lengyel Bernat-Bernard interviewed by Nancy Fisher on 28 August 1998. This testimony interview is available in full online. Part I https://youtu.be/ufxLw-xSEMM?si=WKRsYRUQhuwGkszR and Part II https://youtu.be/Zq1Uh_BiMso?si=M60jDwuu3mYTRKTI

CHAPTER 2

An Experience in Search of a Form: Reading Olga Lengyel's Testimony Through Translation

Peter Davies

Abstract Taking as its starting point the translation and edition history of Lengyel's testimony, this chapter considers the narrative and linguistic resources available to the testifier in the immediate post-war years. It explores the text's transformations and rewritings for new readerships, asking what this means for questions of authenticity and the individual voice of the survivor. Lengyel's text underwent significant restructuring in the passage from French to English, shifting between an emphasis on political resistance and a bourgeois ethics of respectability, all the time seeking to find a form and style adequate to the experience of Auschwitz. The chapter also addresses Lengyel's problematic depictions of female sadism and homosexuality, suggesting that they have a narrative function beyond a desire to attract a readership looking for prurient accounts of camp life.

Keywords Translation · Edition · Collaboration · Narrative · Sexuality

Olga Lengyel's published written testimony, in the specific English version entitled *Five Chimneys: A Woman Survivor's True Story of Auschwitz,*

P. Davies et al., *Olga Lengyel, Auschwitz Survivor,*
https://doi.org/10.1007/978-3-031-82490-6_2

which we have chosen as our point of reference for this study, has an arresting opening paragraph:

> *Mea culpa*, my fault, *mea maxima culpa*! I cannot acquit myself of the charge that I am, in part, responsible for the destruction of my own parents and of my two young sons. The world understands that I could not have known, but in my heart the terrible feeling persists that I could have, I might have, saved them (Lengyel 2000, 11).

The opening words may be familiar to many readers as a reference to part of the Catholic Confiteor, which was until the 1960s spoken by the priest at the beginning of the Latin mass. In this ritual context, it is the commencement of a process of atonement that is public, collective and conducted by and through the priest. Lengyel blends this religious reference with legal language ('acquit myself of the charge'), creating a statement about the complex, multi-layered sense of the term 'to testify' by locating it in two different linguistic contexts and discourse histories. The language of Catholic practices of collective, ritual atonement and the language of legal culpability both suggest overarching social, discursive instruments for defining guilt and innocence; they are here juxtaposed with a sense of individual, moral conscience that neither of them are able to assuage.[1]

This dramatic opening positions the text as a confession born of an urge to tell a difficult personal story and atone for an action: it is a rhetorical claim to trustworthiness through confession of hidden truths, a form that operates in legal and religious contexts. There is, though, a strange instability about this statement: is she really guilty of these deaths, or does she just *feel* guilt? But if the 'world' actually knows she is innocent, then why the need to confess and atone in public? The opening of the English version of *Five Chimneys* raises questions that, as I intend to show here, the text itself does not actually answer in a clear way. Instead, the reader is presented with a sometimes uncomfortable juxtaposition of different genres within a single text, indicating perhaps a struggle to find a register, style or narrative structure that can adequately convey the experience of Auschwitz.

In this chapter, I will argue that Lengyel's text demonstrates the difficulty of formulating testimony at a very early stage (1946/47) and that tracing the translation and edition history of the text, in particular,

---

[1] Thanks to Dr. Paul Parvis for advice on this point.

comparing the French and English versions, can give us important insights into how the survivor formulates and reformulates her experiences in different contexts and for different readerships. Lengyel's text is never finished or closed but bears the marks of a struggle to reconcile conflicting views of selfhood and different demands of publishing contexts. To illustrate this, I discuss questions of translation, rewriting and embellishment, looking at what we gain by reading the texts together, rather than seeing one as the 'translation of' the other.

Mea Culpa Between French and English

Reading this edition, one would not know that it exists in a line of antecedent texts in other languages, as the publication information makes no reference to translation. However, an earlier edition of this English text, entitled *Five Chimneys: The Story of Auschwitz*, positions itself as a translation from French and Hungarian, crediting two translators, Clifford Coch and Paul P. Weiss, with the work (Lengyel 1947a). I discuss the edition history of this text in more detail below, but this earlier edition provides us with editorial evidence for a relationship with other texts that are here considered earlier, perhaps 'originals'.

The claim to a relationship between the texts authorises a standard critical procedure based on comparing 'original' with 'translation' in order to investigate potential 'translation shifts'. We have found no trace of an earlier or parallel Hungarian manuscript, though one may exist, but if we read the opening lines of the French edition of Lengyel's text that was published a year earlier in 1946, we find this:

> Mea culpa, mea maxima culpa! Je me sens responsable de la mort de mes parents et de mes deux fils.
> Ce sont les faits (Lengyel 1946, 17).

> *Mea culpa, mea maxima culpa! I feel responsible for the death of my parents and my two sons.*
> *These are the facts.*[2]

---

[2] For the purpose of comparing the English and French versions of Lengyel's text, I have provided a direct English translation of Lengyel's French text in italics and further indented. I hope that this makes clear the distinction between my translation of Lengyel's French and the (often very different) English version that we are working with in this study, and which I quote with page references. My translations of the French are designed

The French lines are dramatic at the rhetorical outset, but then shift quickly to a more sober language of factual detail, as if at the beginning of a police report or confession: compared with the English version, this is tersely expressed and with a starker contrast between the dramatic opening and the sober promise to set out facts.

The English version provides a translation of the words 'mea culpa', suggesting that the intended readership for this text may well not share a Catholic background. However, by contrast with Lengyel's version, the phrase is usually translated (for example, in the Catholic Encyclopedia) as 'through my own fault': the phrase in the prayer is 'I have sinned ... through my own fault', confirming that the speaker accepts personal responsibility for the transgression of moral law, and will not blame others or any external circumstances. It is a complex process, first acknowledging the law, understanding its relevance for the individual, accepting that a transgression has occurred, thus confirming the validity of the law and then accepting personal fault. The English translation references a more colloquial expression ('it's my fault') that does not necessarily imply that an overarching moral law has been transgressed.

This may be a small distinction, but it is of a piece with other features of the English version, which seems to simultaneously confess to and deny guilt: it expands, intensifies and qualifies the self-accusation, and has a more intensely emotional tone (for example, using the word 'destruction' for the French 'mort'). Oddly, the English version appears to reverse the sense of the Catholic prayer, in which sins are made public and acknowledged by the community: here, the world knows that she is innocent, but she cannot shake off an internal feeling of guilt. The small shift in phrasing from 'je me sens responsable' to 'I cannot acquit myself' is telling: Lengyel and her translator/collaborators could have used the English word 'responsible' here. Instead, she adds a layer of legal discourse, while suggesting that someone else will acquit her as innocent, even though she is unable to do this herself.

But who is the 'world'? This text appears to suggest that the readers, as the 'world', are already aware of her innocence: the text is introduced to us as an account of her inner, psychological struggle with her conscience, and we are positioned as participants in a process of exculpation, forgiveness and acceptance. By contrast, the French text appears to open a debate

to give an impression of the French and are, therefore, not intended to read entirely fluently or idiomatically in English.

about questions of fact: the readers are offered the facts in order to make this judgement.

By contrasting these texts—a procedure that the current English edition denies us, unless we have done some research into its edition history—we identify some crucial differences in how they position themselves and open an interesting field of tension between the two. There are other questions that arise here, which will be explored further in this chapter: in what kind of relationship do the texts stand to each other, and is it possible to locate an authentic moment of original testimony by comparing translations? We might be tempted to look at the French text as the 'original', in the hope that it contains an earlier, and perhaps more 'authentic' testimony statement preceding any elaborations that have appeared in the English: if it is closer chronologically to the events, is it thus more trustworthy?

I feel the temptation to accept the text's opening words as a true expression of guilt and anguish, rather than simply a rhetorical figure drawing on the power of the genre of confessional autobiography in Western culture. It may, of course, be both: drawing on a powerful rhetorical tradition to drive home a truth. The opening of this text seems to perform in a few lines a secularisation of religious notions of confession, proceeding through legal forms into a specific genre of autobiography: it is finding its way to the notion of 'testimony' that we as scholars now work with.

It is not possible to know about Lengyel's motivations for the preoccupations of her text: one can come to tentative conclusions based either on text-internal evidence or on contemporary publishing policies. One could suggest a need for the author to write herself into a story of heroism, rather than passive victimhood, which would explain the way she frames her narrative about being recruited for the camp resistance, or an attempt to find a way of dealing with the seam of self-disgust and abjection that pervades the text, which might help explain the pornographic, misogynistic and homophobic elements. The text also displays a desire to construct a persona of bourgeois respectability that connects her pre-Holocaust family history with the present of writing: though this aspect is clearer in the much later video testimony.

This problematic text presents us with a dilemma that leaves us speculating about authorial intention and reaching for things that we have no access to. I intend, therefore, to take a different angle, confronting the issue of translation head-on. Rather than assuming that one text is dependent on the other—drawing on a host of established modern legal, economic and ideological discourses in order to describe one as 'a translation' of the other—I propose considering the French and English texts alongside each other, as texts that reveal more in comparison than in isolation.

In the next section, I will briefly set out the translation history, as far as it can be established, of the text we now know in English as *Five Chimneys*, and then discuss how I will approach the question of comparison. I then go on to read the translations together, exploring the different structuring of some aspects of the testimony—the account of the Lengyels' deportation, of resistance and questions of sexuality in the camp—and the contrasting linguistic strategies of the two versions. My aim is to show how differently the French and English texts work through the ideas of testifying, guilt, fact and doubt that the opening lines introduce and to demonstrate that there is more to the question of translation and rewriting than simply ensuring that a text attracts readers in a new context.

TRANSLATION AND EDITION HISTORY

The text's origins are rather obscure, which is not unusual for the early written testimonies of newly liberated survivors. We know it was written down in the first months after liberation. The earliest publication that we have is in French, from 1946, but we do not know for certain what was the original language of writing, or even whether it makes sense to talk about an 'original' language. We should assume that the texts arose in collaboration with others: fellow survivors, informants, editors, gatekeepers, translators or linguistic advisors.

Publication policies for translations, and philological approaches to translation analysis, have conservative habits: texts are compared in order to place them in a chronological relation of dependence, with a translated text following from an earlier text, which in the process is transformed into the 'original'. But in the initial period after liberation, many survivors spoke and wrote in different forms and contexts, in multiple languages and sometimes in hybrid forms that the monolingualism of publishing and nation states finds hard to deal with (Gramling 2012). Translators are conceived as people who shift meaning from a pre-existing finished text in one established language to another, rather than as supporters, co-witnesses, co-writers or editors, fellow survivors, language brokers, gatekeepers and/or collaborating language experts, which is what they often are. There is rarely an 'original' testimony.

Critical writing on Lengyel's testimony has shown some confusion about its 'original' language. Myrna Goldenberg writes that 'before the end of December 1945 [Lengyel] sold her memoir under its first title, *Hitler's Ovens*. Published in 1947, *Hitler's Ovens* was written in several languages, revised into Hungarian, and then translated into French. It was very well received and became required reading in French secondary schools' (Goldenberg 2003, 740). Goldenberg also lists several English reviews from 1947. By contrast, David d'Arcy writes: 'After the war, she settled in Paris, where she wrote the memoir *Souvenirs de l'au-delà*, which was published in English in 1947 as *I Survived Hitler's Ovens*. Later editions of the book were retitled *Five Chimneys: A Woman Survivor's True Story of Auschwitz*'. Langer simply writes that her testimony was 'one of the first accounts of that camp to be written and perhaps the first to appear in English, as early as 1947' (Langer 2021, 169).

So there is no consensus about whether a Hungarian version preceded the French or in what relationship the English edition stands to the other texts, or indeed whether they were perhaps all written together at more or less the same time. Goldenberg's and d'Arcy's accounts are mutually contradictory, Goldenberg implying that an English version preceded both French and Hungarian versions, and d'Arcy assuming the opposite. Concrete evidence to resolve this issue is lacking. However, as I show below, there is some text-internal evidence that may allow us to tentatively establish the relationship between the English and French texts, at least in the published form that we have.

The texts appear in a context in which large amounts of survivor accounts are circulating in many languages, and there is no canon of widely read works: the common features of survivor testimony identified by Robert Eaglestone are still developing (Eaglestone 2004), and publications are more often than not formulated as political interventions rather than as contributions to 'memory'. As Sheila E. Jelen sets out in more detail in her contribution, the immediate international context may be the Doctors' Trial at Nuremberg, which ran from December 1946 to August 1947; important memoirs by Jewish former camp medical orderlies like Gisella Perl, Miklós Nyiszli or Lucie Adelsberger were published in this context, contributing to public understanding but also feeding a more prurient interest in stories about Nazi 'medical' experiments. So Lengyel's texts intervene in this urgent discussion, though, as

Sheila E. Jelen shows in her contribution to this volume, they may be influenced by a more trustworthy account by Perl.

Lengyel included a lot of information in her testimony when it was written that was circulating in survivor communities, in order to provide a compendium of knowledge, authenticated by a first-person account, at a time when secure knowledge was scarce. The text is full of statistical information—inaccurate but convincingly presented— that Lengyel claims was available to her at the time, and accounts of events that she may have had no part in (such as the *Sonderkommando* uprising) and that she could only have known about at second hand or after liberation. No subsequent edition of her testimony has taken the time to correct or comment on this information: a failure of editing and historical oversight that tells us as much about the economics of publishing as it does about any interest in maintaining Lengyel's text's status as a contribution to understanding.

The French text appears in the publishing house Éditions du Bateau Ivre in 1946; the already well-known Hungarian writer and translator Ladislas Gara, whom we discuss in the Introduction, is named on the cover, acting as gatekeeper for the text. His role in the text is hard to pin down: the phrase 'traduction hongroise adaptée par Ladislas Gara' is vague, suggesting that his role lay more in correcting and editing a translation than in producing a new French version of an original text. This is another hint at collaborative practices, though it is hard to reconstruct the extent of his role in shaping the French text, rather than just working on the translation. One can assume that Gara was able to support Lengyel's publication in Éditions du Bateau Ivre, where his own novel had appeared.

The earliest English edition gives us some hints about translation. It was published in New York in 1947 by Ziff Davis, at the time better known as a publisher of hobbyist magazines and the important science fiction magazine *Amazing Stories*. Its initial title was *Five Chimneys: The Story of Auschwitz* (Lengyel 1947a) but a new edition appeared a few months later with the more dramatic title *I Survived Hitler's Ovens* (Lengyel 1947b). Translators are not listed in the publication information, but there is an acknowledgement: 'Thanks are also due to Clifford Coch for translating from the French edition of the same work, to Paul P. Weiss for translating the balance from Hungarian'. This is still not absolutely clear, but we appear to be dealing with a composite text made up of elements from the French edition and a Hungarian text, possibly a manuscript, which we have been unable to locate.

The phrase 'translating the balance from Hungarian' implies that everything that was not included in the French text was translated from a Hungarian source text, rather than added for the English edition, but given that the French text also claims to be translated from Hungarian, this seems unlikely. We may assume, therefore, without having final proof, that extra material was added to the text for publication on the US market in 1947. There is a reprint under the title *I Survived Hitler's Ovens* in 1957, around the time that Lengyel fled Cuba (Lengyel 1957), but later editions use the title *Five Chimneys: A Woman Survivor's True Story of Auschwitz*, and are unchanged reprints of this early text, except that translation information is entirely missing. This means that there is no acknowledgement of the text's complex genesis or the involvement of other hands in its creation. The English text now presents itself as the original.

The shifting titles of the different editions reflect different ways in which the text is positioned in the marketplace: the French title suggests a more literary genre, a perhaps ironic reference to mythical journeys to the Beyond, or the Underworld, while *I Survived Hitler's Ovens* feels entirely different, positioning the text with the promise of sensational revelations, and putting more stress on the personal story. *The Story of Auschwitz* removes the personal perspectives, promising the reader a historical account at a time when secure factual information was lacking. The slightly cumbersome current version of the title, *A Woman Survivor's True Story of Auschwitz*, tries to combine all these elements, but stresses the individual story of the survivor rather than the 'story of Auschwitz', reflecting a shift in the way testimony is read and valued away from eyewitness accounts of events and towards a more subjective orientation. The subtitle's emphasis on Lengyel's status as a female survivor re-evaluates the text as a contribution to studies of women's testimony.

In 2021, a new Hungarian version of the text was published, naming the translator Ágnes Stier (*Öt kémény, egy Auschwitzi túlélő igaz története* [*Five Chimneys: The True Story of an Auschwitz Survivor*]: Lengyel 2021). Stier is an established translator of English, and the text appears to be a new translation of the English text, rather than an edition of any original Hungarian manuscript.[3]

---

[3] My thanks go here to Dr. Beatrix Futák-Campbell for her invaluable help with the Hungarian edition. This proliferation of titles in translation is by no means unique: the

It is possible to make some assumptions about the relationship between the French and English texts: the English text is expanded in comparison with the French text, but the exact relationship is hard to establish, and there are some confusing elements. So we should see the French and English versions as two iterations of the same text, produced as interventions in different contexts. It is a compendium of information, statistics, stories and rumours, written for a context in which information was still emerging and under dispute, and perpetrators were being tried: both texts use the individual witness's perspective as a narrative hook and guarantor of authenticity, and both connect the ethical agency of resistance to the gathering of 'reliable' knowledge. I suggest that we look at the texts as parallel interventions, rather than as standing in a relationship of chronological dependence: how do they speak to each other and to their context?

However we perceive the relationship between the French and English texts, there are significant differences that we need to consider; taking translation seriously complicates views of Lengyel's testimony that appoint a single version as an authoritative source, rather than thinking through genre distinctions and the context of publication. Lengyel's text seems to refer to multiple genres in loose, tense juxtaposition: it draws on multiple modes of writing associated with forms of truth telling that are supported by different discursive formations. It is such an early testimony that there is no established genre 'Holocaust testimony' with recognisable features to influence writing. We have seen how the opening paragraph performs a move through religious and legal confessional forms: the text also employs autobiographical, confessional, historical and sociological narrative forms, alongside anecdote, eyewitness report, accusation, adventure, pornography, melodrama, self-analysis, statistics and political commentary. It is a compendium of clashing styles and genres: an experience in search of a form.

Lengyel's text is a telling example of a survivor trying to employ available, familiar or culturally sanctioned modes of writing in order to formulate something about their experiences. We may perhaps find this procedure more calculating than is the case with other survivors trying to find ways of articulating what has happened to them, but exploring Lengyel's testimony in this way gives us an insight into the formation

presentation of Miklós Nyiszli's text undergoes similar swings between sensationalism and soberness (see Davies 2018, 48–49).

of a genre at this early stage. So instead of trying to understand the text in terms of criteria of honesty, as in Sue Vice's distinction between 'fake', 'false' and 'embellished' testimony (Vice 2014), we could, while acknowledging the issues with truth, accuracy and truthfulness, consider the text in terms of Lengyel's public self-positioning in context, how she goes about developing the role of survivor-witness by stitching together genres that promise different kinds of authenticity. It is this fragile textual construction that comes in itself to be considered a model of the genre 'testimony', and I would argue that translation plays a role in this process.

Translation is a process that has a profound effect on the translated text, transforming it into an 'original'. A text is marked as a translation so that it can refer back to a text considered to precede it, establishing a specific kind of relationship between them: how that relationship is defined can vary between historical, cultural and legal contexts, and can be subject to debate and challenge, but the notion of precedence is a defining feature of most conceptions of translation. There are compelling ethical reasons when discussing testimony in translation for insisting on a modern, Western conception of translation that depends on a strong ethical-legal commitment to originality, responsibility, truthfulness, and authenticity, and on a clear distinction between author and translator: these elements are framed in a specific way that positions the translated text in a relationship of dependence on an earlier text, which is considered more original and authentic, 'closer' to the author.

Framing such ethical questions in terms of space and movement (closer to an origin) becomes problematic when we consider a text such as Lengyel's, whose manuscript and language origins are convoluted and hard to reconstruct. We should note though that this complexity only seems convoluted and confusing in retrospect, from the position of an observer motivated by the wish to access—to get closer to—a supposed point of origin, imagined to be clear, direct and authentic, from which the survivor testifies. The complexity is, in fact, quite normal; we just require a conception of translation that can grasp it.

The production of a text that is referred to under specific conditions as a translation contributes to a process by which a text or set of texts with complex origins is stabilised into an original: this is the purpose of the legal and financial framework, displayed in publication information, in which the hands involved in producing a text are clearly labelled as 'author' and 'translator'. Lengyel's text goes further than this: as we have seen, the early French and English editions obfuscate the framework of translation in different ways, and the current English edition disguises its origins in translation and textual complexity. There is now a Hungarian text that may be entirely different from any Hungarian text that Lengyel actually wrote. Translation has helped to stabilise a fundamentally unstable text from the very earliest days of testimony-writing.

If we take a different perspective on translation, one that no longer seeks to identify authentic moments of origin, then we find that we can set aside some of the anxiety produced by our doubts about this text and its origins, and move instead to thinking about what Lengyel's texts actually do: what can we learn from them when read side by side, rather than trying to establish a relation of precedence?

So, returning to the texts' opening words, it is possible to resist the temptation to see the French opening as a more original expression of guilt, which we can isolate by identifying and stripping away later additions in the English text. Instead, we can see them as two differently framed ways of thinking through how to write about the survivor's responsibility in contexts in which there are few established models to draw on. The French version appears more confident, while the English version displays an anxious need to qualify its own terms and appeal to the reader in a rather contradictory way. Both position the writer as a testifier, activating specific genre expectations that are simply placed side by side in the French, whereas the English text articulates or exposes the tension between them.

READING THE TEXTS TOGETHER

The French and English texts appear to be directed at different publishing contexts. The French text appears in a context in which resistance and political commitment is validated, so Lengyel positions herself as a political resister, writing herself into the history of resistance in the camp. She cannot portray herself as a political prisoner, but in line with the text's emphasis on agency and choices, she narrates her deportation to Auschwitz as a result of a positive commitment to go with her husband: she claims to have had the choice whether to join him or not. The account of her time in the camp is structured around the moment of political commitment when she is approached by the resistance and asked to work as a courier: this is what enabled her to gather knowledge about the camp and the extensive statistical information that she shares with the reader.

Besides the story of her resistance activity in Auschwitz, which is foregrounded in the French text, many of the supposedly improbable things that Langer objects to in his essay are only present in the English text. So, a story about a Wehrmacht officer being billeted on her family and warning them about the mass killing of Jews is present in English, as is a complete final chapter that makes some comments about the triumph of hope and human dignity. The French text ends abruptly and rather bluntly with Lengyel's escape from a death march, leaving the ending quite open.

The vast majority of the descriptions of sexualised violence, which the English text is well known for, in particular, the obsessive attention to the notorious female guard Irma Grese, whom Lengyel claims to have known personally, are absent in the French version. The French text does contain a homophobic account of lesbianism in the camp in a faux sociological style, but this is expanded and intensified in the English version. Parts of the English version read like Holocaust pornography and are clearly aimed at a different publishing context to the French text, presumably with commercial considerations in mind. The extra material shifts the text's centre of gravity away from political resistance to a more anxiety-ridden autobiographical self that negotiates and externalises questions of bodily disgust and abjection.

There are stylistic reasons for thinking that the English text may ultimately be derived from the French. For example, a sentence like 'The most poignant problem that faced us in caring for our companions was that of the accouchements' (Lengyel 2000, 113) reads to me like translatese: a Latinate English that arises from the register differences between French-derived words in English and their French cognates. The French text has: 'Le problème humain le plus poignant qui se posât à nous autres, chargées de soigner nos compagnes d' infortune, était celui des accouchements' (*The most harrowing human problem that we others faced, who were charged with caring for our fellows in misfortune, was the problem of childbirth*) (Lengyel 1946, 170). The word 'poignant' in English is a false friend here; the French word describes a far stronger, more immediate feeling. The English text also contains occasional moments of stylistic inappropriateness: for example, in discussing the killing of newborn babies, the French refers to 'le nouveau-né' (*the new-born*)

(Lengyel 1946, 171), while the English has 'the little tike' (Lengyel 2000, 114).

The language of the English version is often intensified in comparison to the French. If we look at the description of the train journey to Auschwitz, which contains a narrative describing how Lengyel and her husband improvised the rescue of a woman who had taken poison, we find a more dramatic narration:

> Sur les rails, un interminable convoi de wagons à bestiaux, plein à craquer de candidats à la déportation, attendait. Les wagons attestaient toutes les origines: Hongrie, Yougoslavie, Roumanie. Dieu sait où ce convoi avait été formé (Lengyel 1946, 20).

> *On the tracks was waiting an interminable convoy of livestock waggons, full to bursting with those selected for deportation. The waggons all testified to their origins: Hungary, Yugoslavia, Romania. God knows where the convoy had been put together.*

> There was a nightmarish quality to the scene. On the tracks, an endless train waited. Not passenger coaches but cattle cars, each filled to bursting with candidates for deportation. We stared. People called to each other fearfully. The insignia on the car indicated their points of origin: Hungary, Yugoslavia, Rumania—only God knew where this train had first been assembled (Lengyel 2000, 15).

The English account of this journey includes passages such as this, that are absent from the French:

> The cattle car had become an abattoir. More and more prayers for the dead rose in the stifling atmosphere. But the S.S. would neither let us bury nor remove them. We had to live with our corpses around us. The dead, the contagiously ill, those suffering from organic diseases, the parched, the famished, and the mad must all travel together in this wooden gehenna (Lengyel 2000, 19).

The account of the transport has a slightly different structure in the two texts. The French version begins with a paragraph that stresses that they were just a small part of a larger machinery, commenting on the 'banality' of the proceedings as an ironic commentary on the distanced, mechanised organisation of the transports:

Ce fut un voyage morne, lugubre, et en somme banal, puisqu'aussi bien son histoire est celle de tous les autres wagons du convoi, et très certainement aussi celle d'innombrables convois partis de tous les coins d'Europe, de France, d'Ukraine, des Pays Baltes et des Balkans, vers la même destination (Lengyel 1946, 21).

It was a bleak journey, gloomy, and all in all banal, since its story is the same as all the other waggons in the convoy, and very certainly also the same as countless other convoys that departed from all the corners of Europe, from France, Ukraine, the Baltic States and the Balkans, towards the same destination.

This paragraph is shifted to the end of the English version, and loses the word 'banal': the narrative perspective shifts here, ensuring that it is clear that they are unaware of the 'big picture':

The trip was incredibly morbid and gloomy, and although the same could have been said of every other car on our train, and indeed, of the innumerable trains from every corner of Europe—from France, Italy, Belgium, Holland, Poland, the Ukraine, the Baltic countries, and the Balkans—which were all moving toward the same inhuman destination, we knew only our own problems (Lengyel 2000, 17).

The intensification of language is a feature of certain translations of Holocaust testimony: the translator seems to be engaging with their own feelings about what is being described (see Davies 2018, 31–38). A specific difference between the French and English texts is the sexualised descriptions of perpetrators and their actions. These aspects are present in the French but are far more extensive and prominent in the English version so that they tip the balance of attention away from the account of Lengyel's resistance activities towards sensationalised descriptions of psychopathy and 'deviance'.

For example, at one point Lengyel narrates an encounter with the SS guard Elisabeth Hasse. Lengyel has asked a criminal prisoner for help in finding her son, and is approached by Hasse, threatening violence; the prisoner protects Lengyel by flirting with the guard: 'La commandante sembla désarmée par l'oeillade que lui lança le criminel, un homme au physique avantageux. Elle éclata de rire. Ma naïveté était vraiment désopilante' (*The commandant seemed disarmed by the flirtatious glance cast at her by the criminal, an attractive physical specimen. She burst out laughing. My naivety was genuinely hilarious*) (Lengyel 1946, 70).

The English version expands this brief scene, adding information about Hasse's appearance and her 'unfeminine' sexuality, and substituting a weary knowledge for the narrator's original naivety:

> The criminal winked at her and the commander seemed to be appeased. He was an attractive physical specimen, while she was a fat, ugly creature. She forgot me and gazed at the criminal intently. Hunger and lust burned in that glance. One understood these things in the camp (Lengyel 2000, 46).

Long, detailed accounts of the sadism and depravity of Irma Grese in the English text build on this sense of the camp as a space of unnatural female sexual depravity and allow Lengyel to present her narrating self as 'normal', possessing the ethical strength to resist temptation and uphold her marriage. Experiences of bodily abjection and self-disgust appear to be externalised and projected onto these scenes, which are staged in such a way as to elicit fascination in the reader while providing space for condemnation and self-exculpation. This aspect is far stronger in the English text, which performs an elaborate, multifaceted defence of heteronormative sexuality, introducing elements that make it a structuring feature of the narrative, which is not in the French text.

Insa Eschebach has discussed this feature of Lengyel's text, setting it in the context of other testimonies that construct a link between female homosexuality and murder, and demonstrating that there is far more to this aspect of the text than simply pandering to a specific market. Homophobic narrative elements act to 'create social distinctions, reinforce group identity and demonstrate moral superiority' among the narrator's in-group (Eschebach 2012, 77). Lengyel's narrative performs these actions on a number of levels, employing different narrative and genre tropes: the story of loyalty to her husband, the story of ethically founded resistance, the projection of bodily abjection onto the *mise-en-scène* of sadomasochism and a faux sociological style that makes a claim to providing an objective description of camp society through analysis of the behaviours of different 'groups' of prisoners. The intensification of these aspects in the English text gives the impression of a writing self that has to struggle harder to maintain its own sense of integrity.

The French text contains a discussion of three 'types' of lesbianism in the camp: those who chose relationships with other women out of necessity, those who brought their sexuality with them to the camp and a third category, which Lengyel considers most problematic:

Je range dans la troisième catégorie celles qui [...] se découvraient des goûts lesbiens par une sorte de mode, d'engouement (Lengyel 1946, 284).

In the third category I put those who [...] discovered lesbian tastes in themselves by a kind of fashion, of infatuation.

Sarah Cushman has pointed out that this statement is likely based on authentic observation: 'Despite Lengyel's obvious distaste, she accurately identified the motivations for lesbianism: personal identity, sex-based segregation, and sexual commodification' (Cushman 2020, 110; see also Hájková 2013). My argument takes a different perspective, looking at the contrasting narrative function of these descriptions in the two versions.

The English text replaces 'engouement' (passion, infatuation) with 'corruption': 'In the third category were those who [...] discovered their lesbian predilections through an association with corruption' (Lengyel 2000, 197–98). The English text also contains a narrative about decadent parties among 'privileged' prisoners and a cross-dressing Polish countess who tries to seduce Lengyel, which serves to connect the depravity and violence of the camp with the sexual licence of the 'decadent' pre-war world: these are representations familiar from literary and pornographic works from Sacher-Masoch onwards. The threatening blurring of gender categories, with women becoming sexual predators and violent sadists, is the key to the narrative world of the English text.

There is a moment in the French text where Lengyel tries to qualify or ironise her condemnation of the decadent prisoner parties, even asserting that they were a form of resistance against a deliberate attempt by the Nazis to repress the prisoners' sexuality (an assertion for which there is no evidence):

Au fond, pourtant, mes révoltes étaient sans fondement. Ces lamentables distractions permettaient un instant à ces malheureuses d'oublier la réalité, et cela valait mieux ainsi. De même, il n'aurait servi à rien de s'indigner devant certaines mœurs amoureuses. Quelles que fussent les intentions des Allemands, il est certain qu'ils n'avaient pas réussi à supprimer l'instinct sexuel chez les internés. Ils étaient parvenus, tout au plus, à les refouler ou à les dévier (Lengyel 1946, 285).

Fundamentally, however, my objections had been unfounded. These deplorable distractions allowed these unfortunate women to forget reality for an instant, and that was worth more. Likewise, it would not have helped to become angry

> *at certain amorous habits. Whatever the intentions of the Germans, it is clear that they had not managed to eliminate the prisoners' sexual instincts. At best, they had been able to suppress or divert them.*

The English version of this paragraph changes the emphasis of the statement as if the narrator cannot bear to make even the concession that the 'deviant' sexuality has been produced by the circumstances of the camp:

> But perhaps my disgust was groundless under the circumstances. The horrible distractions provided a few hours of forgetfulness, and that in itself was worth almost anything in the camp. Besides these parties were better than many other things that took place there. The prisoners, men or women, were frequently abused by the German barrack leaders, among whom was a high percentage of homosexuals and other perverts (Lengyel 2000, 199).

After the narrative of Grese's sexual torture of a prisoner, which follows the description of the party in the English version, Lengyel begins the next chapter with a reassertion of heteronormative sexuality and female devotion: 'During the long months, I did everything possible to find some trace of my husband' (Lengyel 2000, 205). There is no equivalent in the French text.

Lengyel's English narration demonstrates her loyalty to her husband on several occasions: resisting the advances of the Polish countess, showing disgust at sexual excesses and homosexual behaviour and manipulating the story of a Polish escapee called Tadek. The French text merely mentions that she has heard about the escape of this inmate (Lengyel 1946, 211–12), but the English text weaves this story further into the narrative (Lengyel 2000: 60–3 and 138). The Tadek who escapes turns out to be a prisoner who had made advances to her on her first arrival, offering food in return for sex. Lengyel refuses his offer, and Tadek moves on to a different woman, who we later discover has caught syphilis: a cruel punishment for 'immoral' behaviour that the narrator appears to relish (see also Bos 2024, 9–11).

Just before his escape, this Tadek comes to Lengyel to apologise to her: 'Anyway, you cannot hate me any more than I hate and abominate myself' (Lengyel 2000, 138). Thus, Lengyel has written herself into the story of somebody else's heroism, portraying herself as the inspiration for Tadek's moral insight into his own degeneration, which he wishes to atone for. As before, abjection and self-hate are projected onto another character in order to maintain a stable narrating self, while also ensuring that the reader is aware of Lengyel's role as a moral catalyst: this story of atonement picks up the thread of the text's opening words.

Lengyel's textual defence of heteronormative sexuality performs a function on different narrative levels: creating an overarching structure (the story of finding her husband) that is interwoven with the resistance narrative in the English text, ensuring that she is seen to be fulfilling wifely duties under duress rather than just engaging in political activity; establishing a stable narrating self that compensates for the tension between the text's different narrative discourses; supporting a persona of bourgeois respectability that provides a refuge, a link with the past, and an ethical core; and establishing herself as a respectable, loving motherly woman who is able to narrate her story of losing her family and killing babies without self-disgust.

Where the French text locates her choice to resist an explicitly political decision in favour of solidarity, responsibility and agency, the English text includes structuring elements that locate her moral persona in a supposedly pre-political sphere of tradition, bourgeois family life and motherliness. In order to do this, Lengyel's narrating self has to insist even more strongly on her ethical purity and bourgeois respectability, by externalising doubt, guilt, desire and disgust onto other figures. This is the function of the story of Tadek, for example. But the strange uncertainty of the opening paragraph in the English version gives us an insight into the difficulty of this project.

The differences between the versions reveal more than simply pragmatic information about publication contexts, though. If we look at the translation in a way that does not try to trace a lineage for the texts but instead reads them as parallel interventions, then we find that the texts reveal different aspects of the survivor's attempt to create a discursive position from which to speak. The process of (re)formulation, translation and self-translation, editing, collaboration and publishing are as much part of the survivor's 'identity-work' as are the internal narrative structures of the texts themselves (Pollak et al. 2016).

There is more to say about Lengyel's written testimonies than is covered by the question of truth, truthfulness, falsehood, authenticity and inauthenticity. We can see here, at this very early moment, how an author is experimenting with ways of writing a genre—testimony—that is still unstable and in the process of invention. What other genres must a survivor draw on in order to write about such an unprecedented experience? What works and what doesn't? What markets and readerships does a survivor need to deal with in order to be heard at all? What does it mean to say 'I', and who is one speaking on behalf of? Of course, as we set out in the final chapter of this book in our discussion of Lawrence Langer's reading of Lengyel's testimony, it does matter whether the writer is being truthful about her experiences, or had adopted others' experiences as her own; however, understanding the process of composition, translation, reformulation and marketing gives us a clearer view of the genre work and uncomfortable compromises that were necessary in order to testify at all.

References

Bos, Pascale R. 2024. Barter, Prostitution, Abuse? Reframing Experiences of Sexual Exchange During the Holocaust. *The Journal of Holocaust Research*. https://doi.org/10.1080/25785648.2024.2383037.

Cushman, Sarah M. 2020. Sexuality, Sexual Violence, and Sexual Barter in the Auschwitz-Birkenau Women's Camp. In *Agency and the Holocaust: Essays in Honor of Debórah Dwork*, ed. Thomas Kühne and Mary Jane Rein, 105–121. Cham: Springer International Publishing.

Davies, Peter. 2018. *Witness between Languages: The Translation of Holocaust Testimonies in Context*. Rochester, NY: Camden House.

Eaglestone, Robert. 2004. *The Holocaust and the Postmodern*. Oxford: Oxford University Press.

Eschebach, Insa. 2012. Homophobie, Devianz Und Weibliche Homosexualität Im Konzentrationslager Ravensbrück. In *Homophobie Und Devianz: Weibliche Und Männliche Homosexualität Im Nationalsozialismus*, ed. Insa Eschebach, 65–78. Berlin: Metropol.

Goldenberg, Myrna. 2003. Olga Lengyel (1908–2001). In *Holocaust Literature : An Encyclopedia of Writers and Their Work*, ed. Lilian Kremer, 738–741. London: Routledge.

Gramling, David. 2012. An Other Unspeakability: Levi and Lagerszpracha. *New German Critique* 39 (3): 165–187.

Hájková, Anna. 2013. Sexual Barter in Times of Genocide: Negotiating the Sexual Economy of the Theresienstadt Ghetto. *Signs: Journal of Women in Culture and Society* 38 (3): 503–533. https://doi.org/10.1086/668607.

Langer, Lawrence. 2021. 'Memory and Invention in Olga Lengyel's Five Chimneys'. In *The Afterdeath of the Holocaust*, 169–95. Cham: Springer International Publishing.

Lengyel, Olga. 1946. *Souvenirs de l'au-Delà*. Paris: Éditions du Bateau Ivre.

Lengyel, Olga. 1947a. *Five Chimneys: The Story of Auschwitz.* Translated by Clifford Coch and Paul P. Weiss. Chicago: Ziff Davis Publishing Co.

Lengyel, Olga. 1947b. *I Survived Hitler's Ovens.* Chicago: Ziff Davis Publishing Co.

Lengyel, Olga. 1957. *I Survived Hitler's Ovens.* New York: Avon.

Lengyel, Olga. 2000. *Five Chimneys: A Woman Survivor's True Story of Auschwitz.* Chicago, Ill: Academy Chicago Publ.

Lengyel, Olga. 2021. Öt kemény: egy Auschwitzi túlélő igaz története. Translated by Ágnes Stier, Szeged: Lazi Könyvkiadó.

Pollak, Michael, Christian Fleck, Gerhard Botz, and Matthias Pollak. 2016. *Die Grenzen des Sagbaren: Lebensgeschichten von KZ-Überlebenden als Augenzeugenberichte und als Identitätsarbeit.* 2. Auflage. Wiener Studien zur Zeitgeschichte, Band 1. Wien Münster: Lit.

Vice, Sue. 2014. Translating the Self: False Holocaust Testimony. *Translation and Literature* 23 (2): 197–208. https://doi.org/10.3366/tal.2014.0150.

CHAPTER 3

Shadow Selves: Olga Lengyel's Poetics of Identification

Sheila E. Jelen

Abstract This chapter addresses how the close resemblance between Lengyel's account of her participation in acts of infanticide at the women's infirmary in Birkenau Auschwitz and Gisela Perl's and reflects Lengyel's commitment to writing not only a personal story about her own tragic losses, but also the collective account of many women's experiences. As Annette Finley-Croswhite has stated, 'The Jewish womb was a "Holocaust landscape", another kind of killing field where the murderous Final Solution was deployed' (Finley-Croswhite 2021, 103). She continues on to note that 'the gender-based dimension of the Holocaust is largely ignored' (Finley-Croswhite 2021, 103). Through her invocation of a collective experience, in her simple use of the pronoun 'we' as she describes the infanticides that took place in the Jewish women's infirmary at Birkenau, Lengyel may very well have been giving voice to a frequent, but silenced, experience of women in the camps. How, though, does this collective locution, this story about the women who worked at the infirmary with the women who gave birth to live infants at Birkenau, serve Lengyel herself and articulate her own unique experience as a traumatised mother?

Keywords Infanticide · Gisela Perl · Women's infirmary · Birkenau · Collective narration · Trauma

P. Davies et al., *Olga Lengyel, Auschwitz Survivor*, https://doi.org/10.1007/978-3-031-82490-6_3

According to Petra Schweitzer, Olga Lengyel and Gisella Perl (1907–1988), a Hungarian Obstetrician/Gynaecologist who was imprisoned at Birkenau and employed there as a physician, were given nearly identical numbers upon arrival at Auschwitz, with Olga's being 25,403 and Perl's 25,404 (Schweitzer 2016, 70, 76). Both Hungarian Jewish female prisoners at Auschwitz who worked in the Jewish women's infirmary, Olga Lengyel's memoir of her time there came out in French as *Souvenirs de l'au-delà* in 1946, and in English as *Five Chimneys* in 1947, while Gisella Perl's memoir, *I was a Doctor in Auschwitz* was published one year later, in 1948 (Perl 1948). Schweitzer explores the two books within the context of a discussion of the Holocaust and the maternal body; the purpose of her analysis, she says, is to shed light on two texts that were among the first to be published by women immediately after the war but had been largely ignored within Holocaust discourse. Schweitzer elaborates:

> At a time when little attention was given to gender studies, both women concentrate primarily upon female victims. Committed to giving testimony to the Nazi atrocities, both authors narrate personal, individual, and collective experiences, thereby documenting the systematic torture imposed upon the female body, in particular pregnant women and their unborn babies. In the years following the war, these important first-person stories remained on the margins of a vast Holocaust research. (Schweitzer 2016, 69)

This essay will focus on the literary result of Olga Lengyel and Gisella Perl's presumed acquaintance as Hungarian medical professionals enslaved in Birkenau's Jewish women's infirmary. They were, if the numbers provided by Schweitzer are correct, also admitted to Auschwitz in the same transport, one right after the other.[1] Lengyel's account of traumatised maternity in her own life, and in the lives of the women she claims to have worked with at the camp, will be the primary text for our discussion.

Schweitzer is not the only scholar who juxtaposes Perl's and Lengyel's stories as mutually illuminating, and corroborative. In an essay titled 'Fertility in the Camps', Elise Bath similarly reads Lengyel's account of

---

[1] The transport's numbers are missing in the records, but we do know they were issued on Sept. 20, 1944. See Czech (2008, 883).

infanticide committed by the female staff of the Jewish women's infirmary alongside Perl's (Bath 2019, 547–8). Bath frames her reading of the two like Schweitzer, as part of a project of, 'throw[ing] light on female-specific experiences which might hitherto have been ignored' (Bath 2019, 542). These general assertions of the importance of Perl's and Lengyel's accounts within the context of women's reported experiences in the camps as well as the specificity of female experience therein are not in the least surprising. It was, however, only when I encountered Schweitzer's allusion to Lengyel and Perl's purportedly sequential identification numbers at Auschwitz that I was compelled to read their memoirs side by side.

I could not believe my eyes. It was as if they were the same person telling the same experience in different voices, like the double creation stories in the first two chapters of the *Book of Genesis*.[2] Both Perl and Lengyel describe the experience of women being propositioned sexually in exchange for food in the lavatory in Birkenau; they both describe suicide attempts; they both describe their work with pregnant women in the camps. It is, of course, entirely possible that they had similar experiences, having been admitted to Auschwitz at the same time if their purported numbers are correct, and having been conscripted into the medical cohort at the same time, according to each of their independent accounts. Yet, upon reading their narratives, side by side, I couldn't help but ask myself whether their stories so closely resemble one another because one of them has borrowed from the other. More specifically, based on my reading of both texts, it strikes me that Lengyel might be borrowing Perl's story because of the way that each of them narrates the infanticides they committed to save their imprisoned mothers' lives. Lengyel describes this in a chapter, titled 'Accursed Births' devoted entirely to this topic:

> Unfortunately, the fate of the baby always had to be the same. After taking every precaution, we pinched and closed the little tike's nostrils, and when it opened its mouth to breathe, we gave it a dose of a lethal product. An injection might have been quicker, but that would have left a trace and we dared not let the Germans suspect the truth. (Lengyel 2000, 114)[3]

---

[2] See also Bos' discussion of the relationship between Lengyel's and Perl's testimonies in Bos (2024, 7, 10–12).

[3] The translation leaves something to be desired as the use of 'tike' to denote infant in this passage is strangely dissonant.

In contrast, about Yolanda, a fellow prisoner in the camp who came to Auschwitz in the early stages of pregnancy and was protected and shielded by Perl until she gave birth, Perl writes:

> On the third day, Yolanda's little boy was born. I put her into the hospital, saying that she had pneumonia – an illness not punishable by death – and hid her child for two days, unable to destroy him. Then I could hide him no longer. I knew that if he were discovered, it would mean death to Yolanda, to myself, and to all these pregnant women whom my skill could still save. I took the warm little body in my hands, kissed the smooth face, caressed the long hair – then strangled him and buried his body under a mountain of corpses waiting to be cremated. (Perl 1948, 83-4)

This passage, which expresses the horror of a 'choiceless choice' (Langer 1982), articulates quite clearly that the babies were killed by hand, and not by tincture. The murder of this infant is a very personal one, one that Perl commits on her own. But the murder of infants, as described by Lengyel, above, was a collective endeavour, carefully choreographed by a team of caregivers for the moment right after birth, when the baby opened its mouth for its first breath.

The difference between these two accounts raises the question of how the infants were really murdered and whose story is at the heart of this narrative. Lengyel's story sounds a bit unlikely. What was this tincture they dropped in the baby's mouth and why isn't she more specific about it? In fact, where might such a tincture have been consistently procured at the infirmary at Birkenau, which Perl calls, 'a grim joke' (Perl 1948, 80). It seems more likely that the murder of the babies had to be committed by whatever means available, and that meant, in most cases, at the hands of the midwife or doctor, through strangulation, as Perl describes. With Perl being an obstetrician/gynaecologist by profession, and one of 'five doctors and four nurses chosen by Dr Mengele to operate a hospital ward that had no beds, no bandages, no drugs and no instruments' (Brozan 1982), it is easy to assume that she was involved in many if not all the births that took place there and the story of these infanticides is hers to tell. According to Noa Gidron, 'multiple testimonies and memoirs of survivors attest to [Perl's] actions. For example, Lea Friedler, whose mother worked with Dr. Perl, wrote: "Dr. Perl performed several abortions every night, one after another"' (Gidron 2020, 49). About her decision to kill newborns to save their mothers, Perl wrote in 1980 that

'The Hippocratic Oath was, for me, the most sacred thing, a commandment of conscience; every word of the Oath was inscribed deep in my heart' (Perl 1981, 89). Just as Perl interpreted the Hippocratic Oath to mean that she had to do everything within her power to save the lives of the mothers, so too did she interpret Jewish law to arrive at the same conclusion. An observant Jew who vowed to her father that if she pursued a career in medicine, she would do so within the parameters of Jewish law, Perl did her best to maintain that promise, even at Auschwitz. According to Jewish law, if one has to choose between the life of a mother and the life of an unborn child, one must choose to save the mother (Biale 1984, 219–38). Gidron tells us that Perl gave herself the 'moral licence' to kill the infants, even if they already had been born, in light of the extreme circumstances facing the mothers at Auschwitz. Perl casts this choice in the language of resistance: 'I knew that my work had a purpose. Here I was a partisan too, a partisan fighting against the Nazis by saving the lives they intended to destroy' (Perl 1981, 153).

Beyond her own account, Lengyel's presence at these scenes of infanticide has not been documented in others' testimonies. Furthermore, the collectivity of the story told by Lengyel might provide us with one clue as to how her text is constructed. She seeks, perhaps, to tell a collective story—of pregnant women at Auschwitz and their caregivers—as her own story. As Annette Finley-Croswhite has stated, 'The Jewish womb was a "Holocaust landscape", another kind of killing field where the murderous Final Solution was deployed' (Finley-Croswhite 2021, 103). She continues to note that 'the gender-based dimension of the Holocaust is largely ignored' (Finley-Croswhite 2021, 103). Through her invocation of a collective experience, in her simple use of the pronoun 'we' as she describes the infanticides that took place in the Jewish women's infirmary at Birkenau, Lengyel may very well have been giving voice to a frequent, but silenced, experience of women in the camps. How, though, does this collective locution, this story about the women who worked at the infirmary with the women who gave birth to live infants at Birkenau, serve Lengyel herself and articulate her own unique experience as a traumatised mother?

To begin to answer this question, let us consider the story of Ruth Elias, an Auschwitz survivor from Czechoslovakia. In her oral testimony with Claude Lanzmann which is housed at the United States Holocaust Memorial Museum, she discusses the birth of her daughter at Auschwitz.

Josef Mengele, she says, was apprised of the birth and decided to document how long it would take for a healthy newborn to starve to death when kept from nourishment. Elias' breasts were bound, and she was forced to watch her daughter starve for a week. Mengele, she said, had warned her on a particular date that if the baby was still alive the next morning, he would take them both to the gas—baby and mother. That night, Elias says, a female doctor came to her with a lethal injection and told her to give it to her own baby. Elias insisted that she could not kill her own child, but the doctor explained that under the Hippocratic Oath, she could not kill the child either. In the end, according to Elias, she killed her own daughter with the injection (Lanzmann 1979).

The reason this story can only be found in the archives at the USHMM is because Lanzmann did not include it in his monumental 1985 film, *Shoah*, choosing instead to feature Elias very briefly as she discusses her transport from Terezín to Auschwitz.[4] This story of devastated motherhood is not a part of the larger story Lanzmann is trying to tell in his monumental film, a 9.5 hour long film that would seem capacious enough to include at least one story about a uniquely female experience—childbirth and infanticide at Auschwitz. Ziva Postec, the editor of *Shoah*, has stated that the theme of the film is death. I would argue instead, that the theme is the *Sonderkommando*, or the Jewish men who were forced to participate in the machinery of death at a variety of camps throughout Poland (Belzec, Sobibor, Treblinka, Chelmno, Majdanek and Auschwitz). Women are discussed throughout the film by men, but uniquely women's experiences such as childbirth in the camps or the creation of self-help communities, which Judith Tydor Baumel has documented in her studies of women in the camps, are not addressed at all (Baumel 1999). As Schweitzer argued above, it is critical to identify and analyse women's narratives on an individual and a collective level. On an individual level, we encounter those narratives that have historically been hushed up not only by perpetrators but also by victims and their communities; sexual intermingling between Nazis and 'undesirables', for example, was contrary to the Nazi racial codes, so for many years even researchers doubted that Nazi soldiers raped Jewish women (Karpiński and Ruvinsky 2016); and women who were sexually compromised were viewed with suspicion and disdain in survivor communities who were focused on the

---

[4] Lanzmann does include Elias' expanded testimony in his 2015 *Four Sisters*.

rehabilitation of the domestic ideals of marriage and motherhood after the war (Hedgepeth and Saidel 2010). Indeed, Sharon Geva, in her study of female Holocaust survivors in Israel documents the way that women who bore arms in the ghetto resistance movements were expected to conform to the traditional gender roles once they arrived in Israel and began to build new lives for themselves there (Geva 2010, 27–91). Finally, women who suffer from sexual abuse are often reluctant to speak of it, so these experiences go under the radar. The mere suggestion that women's experiences in the Holocaust differed from men's, raised first in the public sphere in the 1980s at a conference at Stern College in New York, catalysed a firestorm of criticism from scholars who insisted that 'identity politics' and feminism had no place in Holocaust Studies (Halkin 1998; Schoenfeld 1998). Speaking collectively of women's experiences may have made it easier for women like Olga Lengyel to discuss her own. Her story, I contend, exists at the narrative intersection of the individual and the collective in that she narrates, in her own voice, the stories of others because she cannot tell her own story directly; her own story becomes subsumed in others' stories as a measure of safety and personal discretion. Perl's acts of infanticide became a collective endeavour in Lengyel's text as a means of hiding her own unique traumas as a mother who lost her own children at Auschwitz.

Putting Lengyel's, Perl's and Elias's accounts of infanticide into dialogue with one another raises some important questions. Must one of the stories be truer than the others? Not necessarily. Inconsistency between versions might simply reflect different circumstances in each case. Maybe Perl is only describing one instance, but subsequently, the caregivers in the infirmary were able to identify a deadly tincture, which Lengyel tells us about in her account. And in Elias's case, we learn that doctors associated with the Czech family camp at Auschwitz were not eager to kill infants at all, and that they were able to provide injections in order to make it easier for mothers to murder the babies themselves.

My questioning of the inconsistencies between the three versions is not oriented around my need for historical accuracy, as much as it is motivated by an interest in the way testimonial texts are constructed, and the psychological and cultural moment this kind of 'borrowing' from another's text to tell a story, might reflect. What were the reasons that Elias would report the appearance of a mysterious, anonymous doctor in her barrack with a shot of morphine, on the eve that she and the baby were to be gassed, when it seems highly unlikely that a doctor would be involved in the murder of a baby whose existence had already been established by the camp authorities? Is this a murder that Elias committed on her own, to save herself? Why would Lengyel say that the babies were killed by a tincture, not acknowledging her own individual role in the drama of infanticide? Finally, why would Perl admit to strangling a newborn infant without any assistance or acknowledgement from others, if she hadn't done it? Of all three accounts, it sounds most likely that Perl's is the *Ur* story, the story that the others are based upon. Even though Elias was presumably in the Czech family camp, and not in the same camp as Perl and Lengyel, it could be that Elias' story of the doctor and the injections, may have been a reconstruction of the event, based on Lengyel's account, after the war, to cover up Elias having chosen to kill the baby herself, on the eve of her gassing. Like Lengyel, Elias may have borrowed others' variations on a story of maternal trauma to make better sense of her own.

But, why even sow doubt about Lengyel's or Elias' versions at all? Let me pause here, for a moment to say that my goal here is not to argue whether Lengyel's testimonies are 'true' or 'false'. Even Lawrence Langer, the most vocal of Lengyel's detractors in an essay that we will address in the Epilogue to this volume, admits that: 'Lengyel was certainly a survivor of Auschwitz and is not constructing a fake memoir' (Langer 2021, 177). Why would one woman tell another's story and call it her own in a narrative of the Holocaust written and published in 1946, just after she was liberated from the camps? To what extent is this a phenomenon that might be understood through a gendered lens, as one that expresses the kinds of repressions and silences that are typical of uniquely women's experiences in the war? Sara Horowitz articulates this orientation to Holocaust narratives well, from the perspective of a fellow literature scholar, when she says, 'While the historians examine documentary, and sometimes physical, evidence to determine what was done, to whom by whom, when, and how, I am interested in the shapes and textures of memories of survivors [...]' (Horowitz 2000, 163).

In her introduction to the German version of Perl's *I was a Doctor in Auschwitz*, Andrea Rudorff points to the overlap between Lengyel's and Perl's narratives and even goes so far as to suggest that a woman named Olga Schwartz who is alluded to in Perl's narrative is Olga Lengyel herself (Rudorff 2020, 8). Perl plays an explicit role in Lengyel's account, as Dr. G, which we will discuss shortly, but I am doubtful that Lengyel actually does correspond to Olga Schwartz in Perl's narrative for the simple reason that her description of Olga Schwartz and the death of Olga Schwartz's husband do not match Olga Lengyel's own report of her husband's death. It is, also, of course, possible that Lengyel's account is the one that deviates from historical reality as I have already suggested above, and that Perl's representation of Olga is actually closer to the truth. In any case, the stakes of my claim that Olga Lengyel appears to have adopted Gisella Perl's story are well laid out by Rudorff. She says: 'Holocaust deniers use every inconsistency to question the validity of entire accounts. Olga Lengyel's and Gisella Perl's accounts have been consistently questioned on the internet by Holocaust deniers' (Rudorff 2020, 28). And earlier, she reminds us that:

> It can be assumed that the people portrayed by Perl, including Olga Schwartz, are not necessarily written in a historically accurate sense, but more as allegories of life in the concentration camp, where she utilizes, themes such as friendship, will to live, struggle of survival, sacrifice, and others like degradation, depression, illusion or also the suffering of mothers after the separation from their children. (Rudorff 2020, 8)[5]

One might ask whether Lengyel does damage to the memory of those individuals who were actually involved in the events she narrates by claiming to have participated herself when she may not have. For purposes of this essay, setting aside the possibility that Lengyel may have been involved in the events she describes even if historians haven't documented it, my question is why she claimed to have done so if she was not, and what that kind of question tells us about Olga Lengyel, about Holocaust memoirs written by Auschwitz survivors in Paris in 1946 and about Auschwitz itself.

In keeping with the interdisciplinarity of the testimony project that brings our group together, in my recently published *Testimonial Montage: A Family of Israeli Holocaust Testimonies from the Cracow Ghetto Resistance* I attempt to model a methodology for approaching a group of interconnected Holocaust testimonies from a literary perspective (Jelen 2024). Throughout my close reading of the audiovisual and textual testimonies at the heart of my study, I document the ways that the testimonies intersect with one another not because I am looking for historical corroboration of well-known events, but because I am looking for what Roland Barthes, in his phenomenology of photography, calls 'punctums'

---

[5] Thank you to Bess Dawson for translating the German for me.

(Barthes 1981, 9). A punctum, according to Barthes, is a wound that is unique to the viewer of a photograph, something that grabs them from within the photograph and engages them in unexpected, and sometimes painful ways. How, I ask throughout my study of the Cracow testimonies, do certain details of each testimony and the individual voices behind them, despite the highly collectivised nature of their subjects' activities during and after the war, jump out at me, or 'wound' me as a scholar of literature (Jelen 2024)?

My work in *Testimonial Montage* was largely inspired by a paradox I faced in writing an earlier book, *Salvage Poetics* where I analyse the role of pre-Holocaust documentary photographs in the construction of popular folk ethnographies of East European Jewish life in post-war America (Jelen 2020). In that book, I dedicate a chapter to the iconic photographs of East European Jews taken by Roman Vishniac in the 1920s and 1930s and compiled into photo books after the Holocaust (Jelen 2020, 217–252). In 1947, the captions Vishniac published with the photographs are concise and primarily limited to the place name where the photograph was taken (Vishniac 1947). In 1983, however, in his *A Vanished World*, the captions for those same photographs are quite lengthy and detailed, telling us the names of his subjects and vignettes about each of them, as well, at times, accounts of how Vishniac came to know them and what his interactions with them were like (Vishniac and Mazal Holocaust Collection 1983). In my chapter on Vishniac, I explored the evolution of the captions and tracked the development of Vishniac's auto-ethnographic voice or his premise that he was from the same world inhabited by his photographic subjects when, indeed, he came from a very different world and in most cases didn't even speak their language. To get the rights to republish Vishniac's images in my book, I was required to send my chapter to Vishniac's grandson, Benjamin Schiff, an emeritus professor of Politics and Law at Oberlin College, who was concerned that scholars would reproduce his grandfather's fanciful stories as fact, both in the captions to the photographs, but also in his own personal history. Vishniac claimed, for example, in a *New Yorker* profile on him that was published in 1955 that he had graduated from medical school, when he hadn't (Kincaid 1955). Indeed, when *A Vanished World* was published, the book's editor, Michael de Capua, insisted that Vishniac's lengthy and very detailed captions precede the images in their own special section, because he was certain they were mostly fabricated, and he didn't want them to be too easy to link to any individual photograph

(Newhouse 2010). My interest in *Salvage Poetics*, however, lay precisely in that very disjuncture between the captions and the photographs. I wasn't concerned that Vishniac was prevaricating as much as I was fascinated by the narrative he chose to craft in conjunction with the photographs, and why he fictionalised their subjects.

In a similar vein, what is it about Perl's story that seems to strongly compel Lengyel to organise her narrative around both it and the person of Perl herself? As we know from the opening pages of Lengyel's memoir, she feels that she had a hand in killing her older child. Upon arrival at Auschwitz, she told her older son who had already been selected to enter the camp, to go with his younger brother and their grandmother, Lengyel's mother, to the gas chambers, without realising where they were headed. What she thought she was doing was sparing her older child hard labour and sending him off to a camp for the elderly and for children where they would rest and receive adequate nutrition (Lengyel 2000, 24). She relives this experience throughout her book by closely identifying with the decision of the camp gynaecologist, Gisella Perl, also from Transylvania, to terminate pregnancies and to kill infants, when necessary, in order to save the mother's life.

It is as if to save her own life, Lengyel had to do away with her own children. She even re-enacts the trauma of being a mother killing her own children in the story she tells of a little boy Thomas whom the Nazis decided to kill alongside other small children through 'washing', or bathing them and then freezing them to death, in an effort to scrimp on bullets and gas. Olga claims to have been part of the group of women who, with compassion and sorrow, facilitated the death of those children, but she reminds her reader that they had no choice but to follow orders if they wanted to remain alive (Lengyel 2000, 225–7).

In noting the purported close proximity of Lengyel's and Perl's numbers, and in reading the two memoirs alongside one another, I realised that perhaps what Lengyel is doing is telling a story about traumatised maternity in the camp by becoming, for large segments of it, part of the story told by Gisella Perl, a Birkenau doctor who was witness to traumatised maternity day in and day out at the Birkenau Jewish women's infirmary as she killed babies to save mothers. Kyra Schuster, a curator at the United States Holocaust Memorial Museum has identified a phenomenon of 'acquired memory' among survivors viewing photographs of the Holocaust. Survivors, she says, often see themselves in photographs where they do not actually appear (Jelen 2023). It seems to me that by doing this, they are placing themselves into the documented history of the war because photographs, whether or not they should be, are viewed as a form of incontestable documentation. Lengyel might be aligning herself with another 'documented' account of infanticide in Auschwitz in order to place her own experiences as a mother who, as she perceived it, sent her children to their deaths, externalising her trauma, and to some extent, justifying her own actions.

While Perl never mentions Olga Lengyel (though she mentions other Olgas, as described above), at several junctures, Lengyel mentions Perl, or Dr. G, as she calls her, in her memoir:

> For six months I shared the minute space of Room 13 with five persons. Dr. 'G' was, perhaps, the most interesting of my companions. She was a doctor from Transylvania who, to an extent that was positively unhealthy, refused to reconcile herself to the fact that she was no longer living her old life of pre-Auschwitz days. Every evening she informed us that the Blocova had invited her to tea, and described the incident as though it were one of those elegant tea parties she had known before the war. We knew what the tea party had been. What kind of tea could anyone have in this place? But the doctor insisted on embellishing and glamorizing everything about her. (Lengyel 2000, 145)

Later, Lengyel writes, 'We had no chairs. The only places to sit were on the two lower bunks, the beds of Dr. G and the dentist. These two intelligent women, who probably had been excellent housewives, sobbed like children if we sat on their beds' (Lengyel 1983, 147). Further along, she tells us,

> Dr. G, who was a good doctor, tried to make her dream world real. She kept a maid, a luxury only the blocova were offered. Every morning, before Dr. G got up, one of her patients came in, cleaned the doctor's shoes, tidied her clothes, and made her bed. Dr. G even had a silk coverlet. To avoid our jealousy, she later got one for each of us; but they were ragged and of inferior quality. (Lengyel 2000, 149)

We learn, as well, from Olga that 'Dr. G was always trying on dresses. She got them on the black market or as gifts and had them altered. Toward the end of our captivity, when we could hear the Russian guns, Dr. G remarked, "Well girls, the time has come for me to have a traveling costume made"'. 'We laughed', Olga says in *Five Chimneys*, 'yet we were grateful to her. That intense femininity of hers provided us with many entertaining moments'. Finally, she tells us, 'Dr. G needed praise to keep her dream world going' (Lengyel 1983, 150).

Indeed, in her own memoir, Gisella Perl talks about a game she played with herself and with her friends, a game that she claims spread throughout the women's camp. The game is called 'I am a Lady' and what it entails is the women saying, 'I am a Lady' and then articulating who they used to be in their former lives, and what they aspire to return to. In Perl's case, therefore, she would say to herself, 'I am a lady, a woman doctor in Hungary' (Perl 1948, 58–9). I would argue that Olga's Dr. G, though she renders her in a somewhat absurd form, is the model for Olga's own 'dream world'. In her 'dream world', she falls into the good graces of Dr. Klein, an ethnic German doctor from Transylvania who served as the leading Doctor at Birkenau until the summer of 1944 and enables her to participate in the women's medical corps and to re-enact, again and again, the sacrifice of her sons. In her 'dream world', she participates in the *Sonderkommando* action in 1944 to blow up the crematorium. In her 'dream world', she is able to maintain agency and dignity at Auschwitz, being recognised as the wife of a famous Transylvanian doctor, even by her torturers and using that privilege to save women's lives, both in the delivery room, but also by other means because of her close relationship with Dr. Klein. In the case of the latter, she convinces Dr. Klein to spare the lives of many of the women in Block 25, or the Charnel House at Birkenau who were awaiting gassing, and she procures from him loads of medications for use in the women's infirmary, even inspiring the rage of the infamous Irma Grese (Lengyel 2000, 106).

To what extent are these stories true? I can't say. What I can say, however, is that Olga Lengyel's primary trauma, the 'mea maxima culpa' with which she begins her account, is the unknowing murder of her older son. Even the identity of her children is up for grabs, if truth be told, as in her book she calls one Tomas and one Arvad, while in her 1998 Shoah Foundation testimony she says that her older son's name is Tomas Arvad and she calls her younger son (pulled, according to her, out of the gutter and adopted by her family) David. Indeed, the parenthetical remark I just made about David's origins can be contested as well, I believe, because Lengyel claims that she and her mother were active and influential philanthropists and volunteers at a local orphanage in Cluj (Shoah Foundation 1998). Why, then, would she pull a child out of the gutter and adopt him instead of taking him to the orphanage? Perl too tells a story about adopting one of her patients, a teenage girl who was the victim of incest (Perl 1948, 20–4). Could it be that Lengyel adopts even the story of adoption from Perl because of its powerful message about maternity?

One of the texts I frequently teach in my 'Representing the Holocaust' class is *Auschwitz and After* by Charlotte Delbo (Delbo 1995). *Auschwitz and After*, I teach my students, is an example of a Holocaust memoir that is told in many voices, from many perspectives, in order to create a collective reckoning with incarceration at Auschwitz. Delbo, deported to Auschwitz in 1943 with a group of 230 French women, had been arrested because of their participation in the French resistance. She returns again and again throughout her book to the group of women who helped her to survive, reifying Judith Tydor Baumel's important observations about women's self-help societies in the ghettos and the camps (Baumel 1999). Delbo doesn't just talk about the group experience, however; she ventriloquises women throughout the memoir, taking on their voices in order to tell a particular kind of women's story. In the opening pages of her memoir, for example, we see this short poem:

My mother
She was hands, a face
They made our mothers strip in front of us
Here mothers are no longer mothers to their children. (Delbo 1995, 12)

Delbo speaks here, in the first-person singular, about her mother being stripped before her at Auschwitz. But Delbo, being a non-Jewish prisoner, was not at Auschwitz with her mother. She takes on the voice of a Jewish woman, a woman deported with her family, and presumably her mother, to address the dehumanisation of women, and particularly mothers, in the welcome ritual at Auschwitz.

Olga Lengyel was at Auschwitz. Whether she was one of the medical corps, whether she was a member of the underground, whether she had a son David who was picked up off the street—all of this is hard to ascertain. I would like to conclude, however, with one moment in her oral testimony which I believe sums up the particular agenda she may have been pursuing. In describing her arrival at Auschwitz and her misunderstanding about where she was sending her son, she turns aside and says: 'All the inmates that were taken to the concentration camp had the same history what [sic] I had' (Shoah Foundation 1998, Part 1: 1 hr 31 mins).

What can Lengyel mean? Perhaps she feels that she is testifying not just for herself, but like Delbo, for everyone in her circle of prisoners. At the same time, her own story, the story of her parting from her sons, the story, in a sense of her killing of her own son, is a story that she keeps replaying again and again in her own very individual experience of Auschwitz. And her peer, Dr. G, or Gisella Perl, an officially appointed physician in the Jewish womens' infirmary at Birkenau, had the perfect means of articulating this experience at her own disposal—the experience, over and over again, of killing the living children of the mothers at Auschwitz, children whose warm, heavy bodies came issuing out of their mothers and were subsequently strangled, according to Perl, and disposed of, so that their mothers might have one more day in the kingdom of death.

I am not arguing here that Lengyel stole others' stories. Rather, I believe that she borrowed them to articulate her personal pain. Writ large this is not so very different from what Bruno Grosjean (Benjamin Wilkomirski) did when he took on the identity of a child survivor of the Holocaust to articulate the pain of being separated from his mother and adopted by allegedly unloving parents in early childhood (Mächler and Woods 2001). Of course, while Wilkomirski was not a survivor at all, and Lengyel was, what they had in common, in essence, was borrowing other people's stories to articulate their own profound pain. Drawing on Sue Vice's distinction between false and embellished testimonies, it seems to me that Lengyel's testimony might be considered embellished (Vice 2014). In the case of Delbo, I would not say she was borrowing others' stories to articulate her own pain as much as she was borrowing others' voices in order to articulate their pain after it became impossible for them to articulate their own. The radical similarities between Lengyel's and Perl's two stories might have been a function of Olga playing Dr. G's game: 'I am a lady, a mother of sons in Hungary'.

Another way to look at this, I would argue, is to consider the moment in which Olga Lengyel was writing—in Paris right after the war. In France during that period, those who were speaking about their experiences in the camps were liberated members of the underground, like Delbo, who had been arrested and deported. Lengyel's story of survival, therefore, would fit more easily into her place and moment if she too were to identify as a member of the underground—if not the French resistance, then the underground at Auschwitz, as she does. Perhaps even more to the point is the fact that when she was writing *Five Chimneys*, presumably between 1945 and 1946, The Nuremberg Trials were being held, and the few testimonies by witness-survivors which were being given, were being given for a collective reckoning. Furthermore, the Doctor's Trials at Nuremberg took place from 1946 to 1947, and the paradoxical role of physicians in the camps became a focal point for the depravities of the war within public discourse. In fact, Perl herself was under threat of prosecution for collaboration after the war because of her role as a doctor at Birkenau (Rudorff 2020, 33–35). Of the Jewish doctors employed in the camp, Jolanda Weinberger tells us about 'Dr. Dorota Lorska, a Polish Jewish inmate doctor in Block 10, [who] described the four "degrees of collaboration" faced by medical personnel working within its walls: explicitly refusing an order, refusing an order by not carrying it out, executing an order, and executing an order with zeal' (Weinberger 2020, 138).

Lengyel's adoption of a medical theme in her text, with the help of the experiences that she may have shared, in part, with Perl, but which she elaborated upon in ways that may not be entirely congruent with her own activities at Auschwitz, tunes into a collective experience of coming to knowledge about the perversions of compassion and authority characteristic of the conduct of Nazi physicians. While Perl was by no means a Nazi physician, even her own comportment as a doctor who killed infants in order to save mothers, has been scrutinised and challenged in the discourse.[6] Lengyel's guilt over not having been able to better protect her own children is perfectly articulated in her identification with the 'killer' doctor, even if that doctor was a Jew who, by her own account, was trying to save the lives of mothers by killing their babies. As mentioned above, Lengyel starts her book with the words 'mea culpa, mea maxima culpa'. What better way to combine guilt with grief than to tap into the experience of that very figure—the doctor—who best articulated the paradoxes of the killing machine that employed the most highly educated to do its darkest and most dastardly bidding?

Olga Lengyel, a Hungarian Jewish Auschwitz survivor, bereaved of her parents and her two sons upon arrival at Auschwitz, as well as her husband in the course of his work as a prisoner doctor at Auschwitz, wrote one of the first and only accounts of the experiences of pregnant women and their newborn infants at Auschwitz. Representing the 'gynaecological Holocaust' and the 'Holocaust landscape of the womb'

---

[6] In private conversation with a colleague, I was told how horrifying it is that Perl has been turned into a hero after having murdered so many infants and 'collaborating' with the Nazi Doctors.

in 1946, Lengyel tapped into experiences that, to this day, are rarely to be found in the hundreds of thousands of testimonies that have been gathered by the major archives, such as the Fortunoff Archive at Yale, the Shoah Foundation at USC, the United States Holocaust Memorial Museum and Yad Vashem, among others. The question of her personal claim to the stories she tells raises the issue of whose stories she is telling and why she tells them the way she does in her particular post-Holocaust place and moment. My conclusion is that Lengyel is telling her own very personal story about the loss of her sons at Auschwitz through the story of Gisella Perl's infanticides, and in so doing, Lengyel also provides a point of access to stories about women's experiences in Auschwitz that have yet to be fully researched and understood.

REFERENCES

Barthes, Roland. 1981. *Camera Lucida: Reflections on Photography*. 1st American. New York: Hill and Wang.

Bath, Elise. 2019. Fertility in the Camps: An Exploration of Female Fertility as Reported in Concentration Camp Memoirs. *German Life and Letters* 73 (4): 541–555.

Baumel, Judith Tydor. 1999. Women's Agency and Survival Strategies During the Holocaust. *Women's Studies International Forum* 22 (3): 329–347.

Biale, Rachel. 1984. *Women and Jewish Law: An Exploration of Women's Issues in Halakhic Sources*. New York: Schocken Books.

Bos, Pascale R. 2024. Barter, Prostitution, Abuse? Reframing Experiences of Sexual Exchange during the Holocaust. *The Journal of Holocaust Research*. https://doi.org/10.1080/25785648.2024.2383037.

Brozan, Nadine. 1982. 'Out of Death, A Zest for Life'. *The New York Times*.

Czech, Danuta, and Walter Laqueur. 2008. *Kalendarium der Ereignisse im Konzentrationslager Auschwitz-Birkenau 1939–1945. Translated by Jochen August, Nina Kozlowski, Silke Lent, and Jan Parcer*, 2nd ed. Reinbek bei Hamburg: Rowohlt.

Delbo, Charlotte, and Charlotte Delbo. 1995. *Auschwitz and After*. New Haven London: Yale Univ. Press.

Finley-Croswhite, Annette. 2021. 'Un(B)Earable: Pregnant Bodies and Obstetrical Genocide'. In *Recognizing the Past in the Present: New Studies on Medicine Before, During, and After the Holocaust*, 103–24. New York: Berghahn Books.

Geva, Sharon. 2010. תילארשיה הרבחב האושה תורוביג :העודי אלה תוחאה אל / *El ha-aḥot halo yedu'ah: giborat ha-Shoah ba-ḥevrah ha-Yiśre'elit*. תרדס דרס. ‎ . Sidrat

Migdarim; Variation: Migdarim. [ביבא-לת] : דחואמה קוביץ, [2010][Tel Aviv] : ha-Ḳibuts ha-me'uḥad.

Gidron. 2020. 'Jewish Women Medical Practitioners Who Rescued Fellow Jews during the Holocaust'. *Nashim: A Journal of Jewish Women's Studies & Gender Issues*, no. 36: 39. https://doi.org/10.2979/nashim.36.1.04.

Halkin, Hillel. 1998. Feminizing Jewish Studies. *Commentary* 105 (2): 39.

Hedgepeth, Sonja M., and Rochelle G. Saidel. 2010. *Sexual Violence Against Jewish Women During the Holocaust*. Chicago, UNITED STATES: Brandeis University Press. http://ebookcentral.proquest.com/lib/kentucky-ebooks/detail.action?docID=1084919.

Horowitz, Sara R. 2000. Gender, Genocide, and Jewish Memory. *Prooftexts* 20 (1–2): 158–190.

Jelen, Sheila E. 2020. *Salvage Poetics*. Wayne State University Press.

Jelen, Sheila E. 2023. '"Recognize Somebody?" Post-Holocaust Photographic Recognitions'. USHMM.

Jelen, Sheila E. 2024. *Testimonial Montage: A Family of Israeli Holocaust Testimonies from the Cracow Ghetto Resistance*. Lanham: Lexington Books.

Karpiński, Franziska, and Elysia Ruvinsky. 2016. 'Sexual Violence in the Nazi Genocide: Gender, Law, and Ideology'. In *Genocide*, 149–74. Amsterdam: University Press. https://doi.org/10.1515/9789048518654-008.

Kincaid, Eugene. 1955. 'The Tiny Landscape.' *The New Yorker*, July, 31–56.

Langer, Lawrence L. 2021. 'Memory and Invention in Olga Lengyel's Five Chimneys'. In *The Afterdeath of the Holocaust*, edited by Lawrence L. Langer, 169–95. The Holocaust and Its Contexts. Cham: Springer International Publishing. https://doi.org/10.1007/978-3-030-66139-7_9.

Lanzmann, Claude, dir. 1979. *Claude Lanzmann Shoah Collection, Interview with Ruth Elias*. https://collections.ushmm.org/search/catalog/irn1003912.

Lengyel, Olga. 2000. *Five Chimneys: The Story of Auschwitz*. Chicago: Academy Chicago Publishers.

Mächler, Stefan, and John E. Woods. 2001. *The Wilkomirski Affair: A Study in Biographical Truth*. New York: Schocken books.

Newhouse, Alana. 2010. 'A Closer Reading of Roman Vishniac'. *The New York Times Magazine*. https://www.nytimes.com/2010/04/04/magazine/04shtetl-t.html

Perl, Gisella. 1948. *I Was a Doctor in Auschwitz*. Lanham, Maryland: International Universities Press.

Perl, Gisella. 1981. 'Shevu'at Hipokrates Vesidur Hatefilah'. In *Zakhor: Kovetz Ti'ud Lemesirut Nefesh Begei Haharigah*, 89. Bnei Brak: Agudat Zakhor beYisrael.

Rudorff, Andrea. 2020. 'Einführung in die deutsche Ausgabe'. In *Ich war eine Ärztin in Auschwitz*. Wiesbaden: Marix Verlag.

Schoenfeld, Gabriel. 1998. Auschwitz and the Professors. *Commentary* 105 (6): 42.

Schweitzer, Petra M. 2016. 'Embodied Existence of Mothers: Gisella Perl and Olga Lengyel'. In *Gendered Testimonies of the Holocaust: Writing Life*, 70. 76. Lanham: Lexington Books.

Vice, Sue. 2014. '"False" and "Embellished" Holocaust Testimony'. In *Textual Deceptions: False Memoirs and Literary Hoaxes in the Contemporary Era*, 142–202. Edinburgh: Edinburgh University Press.

Vishniac, Roman. 1947. *A Pictorial Record*. New York: Schocken Books.

Vishniac, Roman, and Mazal Holocaust Collection. 1983. *A Vanished World / Wiesel, Elie,; 1928–2016,; Writer of Foreword*. New York: Farrar, Straus & Giroux.

Weinburger, Ruth Yolanda. 2020. 'Jewish Female Medical Defiance in Block 10'. *Nashim: A Journal of Jewish Women's Studies & Gender Issues*, Jewish Women Medical Practitioners in Europe Before During and After the Holocaust, 36: 138.

Website (last accessed March 2024)

Olga Lengyel Bernat-Bernard interviewed by Nancy Fisher on 28 August 1998. This testimony interview is available in full online. Part I https://youtu.be/ ufxLw-xSEMM?si=WKRsYRUQhuwGkszR and Part II https://youtu.be/ Zq1Uh_BiMso?si=M60jDwuu3mYTRKTI

CHAPTER 4

Negotiating Authenticity and Authority in Olga Lengyel's Testimonies

Hannah Holtschneider

Abstract This chapter compares Lengyel's narrative strategies in her written and oral testimonies in relation to the different contexts of publication to gain a better understanding of Lengyel's sustained quest for authority over her experiences. Hannah Pollin-Galay's concept 'ecologies of witnessing' helps demonstrate the adaptation of testimonial narrative to the vastly different contexts of the immediate post-war years and late 1990s America. Focusing on the narrative of three episodes—deportation, resistance and liberation—the chapter suggests that a close reading of and listening to Lengyel's words in French and English yields insights in relation to the following: a survivor's need to maintain narrative authority; the encoding of gender-based violence in narrative and in the study of testimony across several decades and about the close links between Lengyel's narrative and herself.

Keywords Authority · Sexual violence · Narrative strategy

As we have seen, Lengyel published several versions of her memoir, first in French, then in English, with later translations into various other languages, making her testimony available globally. One way to understand the repeated, slightly altered, but never completely re-written editions of her text, is as attempts to craft her experiences into a more stable form, to make order out of the chaos of the circumstances she experienced. Lengyel may have exercised some control over all editions of her text, while also having to work with editors. Yet the lack of decisive editorial changes by publishers, such as fact-checking and stylistic suggestions to lend the text fluency, suggests that editors, for whatever reason, refrained from such engagement. This is interesting in its own right, but not the main concern of my chapter. Rather, I take my cue from Peter Davies' characterisation of Lengyel's memoir as 'a compendium of clashing styles and genres: an experience in search of a form'. If we read Lengyel's testimony not for establishment or confirmation of historical facts, but as a series of iterations in which she sought to process her experiences for herself and for her changing audiences, we can approach the various, slightly altered, editions of her book as testament to the ways in which her experiences keep needing to be reprocessed, or revisited with each edition.

Reading her memoir together with her video testimony given to the USC Shoah Foundation fifty years later opens the opportunity to consider changes in how Anglophone societies relate to Holocaust survivors. Recorded in 1998 the format of the video testimony follows the standardised questionnaire of the USC Shoah Foundation and thereby does not permit Lengyel completely to structure her own narrative. She does, however, take control of where she places emphasis and how she expands or refuses to speak on the topics asked about by her interviewer. Historiographically, paying close attention to the (changing) voice of a single survivor, I would argue, can yield insights into the cultures of the survivor's origin and the development of 'survivor cultures' since the 1980s (see, in particular, Pollin-Galay 2019). Lengyel, in the late 1940s, is a trailblazer of a new genre or kind of writing—Holocaust testimony or memoir; she is part of shaping its early form. In 1998, she resisted the standardisation of narrative as proposed by the USC Shoah Foundation in the 1990s (see Jeges 2015, 234f.).

Drawing on Hannah Pollin-Galay's concept 'ecologies of witnessing' (Pollin-Galay 2019), Lengyel's words allow insights into the processes of witnessing. 'Ecologies of witnessing' refers to the microcosm constituted by the social, material, imaginary, intellectual, political and cultural context in which humans live and make sense of their lives (Pollin-Galay 2019, 2). 'Ecologies' are complex and sensitive entities that constantly change in response to internal and external stimuli and thus a helpful metaphor to describe the relationships between witness and audience when testimony is uttered. We can observe changes in the way Lengyel approaches her testimony in 1946 in French, how she rewrites it in English in 1947, and how she responds to the opportunity to narrate her life in the standardised video format of the USC Shoah Foundation in 1998 (see also Jeges 2015, 236). From our vantage point, and in contrast to Lengyel's aim in 1946, her testimony today transmits not only her experiences, but testifies also to the cultural contexts that shape her life narrative in 1946, in 1947 and in 1998.

I read Olga Lengyel's testimonies as part of a consistent claim to agency over her own life and as part of a continued effort to gain clarity about her cultural affinity with Germany and Germans and the total destruction of this cultural identification. The 1946 French publication *Souvenirs de l'au-delà* (Lengyel 1946), in particular, seeks to inform the world of the crimes she witnessed and to which she was subjected, of her outrage at the criminals who murdered her family, and it functions as a way of first processing her experiences and sense of responsibility for the murder of her mother and oldest son by writing them down. This same aim is still visible in the 1947 English edition published by Ziff Davis, and which forms the basis of the 1959 re-issue by Granada Publishing (reprinted as Lengyel 1985) and further reprints, now most accessible in print from Academy Chicago Publishers (Lengyel 2000).[1] Central to Lengyel's writing in the 1940s and to her oral testimony in 1998 is the establishment of an authoritative and authentic self, aware of her social position, in conversation with world events and in command of her fate. She communicates to her readers and listeners a coherent and steadfast personality with an independent agency that makes decisions that influence her fate during persecution, deportation, imprisonment and liberation. Written and oral testimonies do this in different ways, but Lengyel's narrative strategy across both pieces is consistent and aims towards the same goal: preserving a sense of self and control over how her life is narrated (see also Jeges 2015, 237f.).

---

[1] I am working with the French publication of 1946 and with the two English editions of 1947 and 1959. It is possible that editions into other languages also reveal small alterations to the narrative, but engaging across a wider range of translations is beyond the scope of this chapter. I quote from the Academy Chicago Publishers reprint of 2000, highlighting divergences with earlier English language editions as relevant, and compare with the French edition from 1946.

Agency

Those who became victims of the Holocaust made meaningful decisions throughout their lives, asserting agency in historical circumstances that were designed to, and in reality did, take away their ability to exert control over their fate. In the case of Olga Lengyel and her family, we have no surviving documentation about her decision-making at the time the events of deportation and imprisonment unfolded. This, obviously, presents us with the difficulty of retracing her decision-making process in 1944/45, but it does leave us with autobiographical recollections over which she had some control. I am primarily interested in tracing how Lengyel articulates her decision-making and sense of agency in hindsight at two points in her life, in historical contexts removed from that of her upbringing and for radically changed audiences. Doing so will enable a better understanding of the 'ecologies of witnessing' relevant to understanding the testimonial statements Lengyel chose to make.

Deliberate narrative choices reflect Lengyel's decision to foreground a consistent moral personality with independent agency in her memoir, and account for the religious framing of the opening passage of her book. As we will observe, Lengyel takes control of her narrative again when she expands her account of her pre-war life in the video testimony (contrary to the directive of the USC Shoah Foundation and the desire of her interviewer); she presents a short narrative of her experiences during imprisonment in Auschwitz and expands the section addressing liberation and the chaos of the end of the war, appearing to voice the trauma of this period for the first time. Lengyel also conceals her real age and her second marriage, again claiming ultimate authority over her life narrative.

Throughout, Lengyel maintains a strong sense of purpose, indicated by the conclusion of her memoir where she states:

> I have tried to carry out the mandate given to me by the many fellow internees at Auschwitz who perished so horribly. This is my memorial to them. [...] Even as I pen my last words, figures rise before me and mutely plead that I tell their stories, too. I can resist the men and the women, but there are the phantoms of the little children ... the little snowmen ... (Lengyel 2000, 225)[2]

---

[2] The entire liberation narrative is missing in the French edition, and there is no post-script which, in the English editions is entitled 'I still have faith'.

As is evident from the discussion in all our chapters, it is clear that Lengyel's memoir narrates more than she experienced or witnessed herself, that she embellishes what she narrates and that she invents improbable episodes. While we cannot be sure why she elaborated her testimony in the ways she did, we can relate her narrative choices to the specific post-war situation she found herself in. Thus, the reporting of things Lengyel neither experienced nor witnessed can be understood as part of a collective effort commonly seen in early Holocaust testimony, namely to inform a wider public about the Holocaust in the absence of easily accessible sources of information and a not-yet-established social discourse about the genocide. Here the context in which she made decisions of what to tell and how to tell indicates a particular perspective on her readers as people who need first-hand information that exceeds personal experience and integrates the survivor narrative with broader interpretations of the atrocities suffered. This is significant in relation to the immediate post-war years where survivor testimony in the courtrooms of the International Military Tribunal was often not seen as sufficiently detailed or was dismissed as unreliable evidence, and where survivors did not find receptive audiences in society for their experiences. Lengyel's book, therefore, can be seen to mobilise accepted techniques of giving evidence, such as drawing on statistics and reports, giving names and locations and integrating the direct experiences of herself and her cohort of prisoners with the wider context of the progress of the war, thus making her camp knowledge relevant to larger frames of reference.

These testimonial strategies assert independent agency and project an ability to author her life and to assign meaning to experiences in ways that lead Lawrence Langer to accuse Lengyel of being an unreliable narrator, of embellishing and fabricating aspects of her memoir, particularly her insistence on being the architect of her own fate (Langer 2021). However, if we see Lengyel's book within the 'ecology of witnessing' in 1946/47, an opportunity opens to consider that she narrated as she did to convey her experiences and imprint their relevance on an audience that had to come to grips with the war crimes trials and the evidence of the camps. At the same time Lengyel's writing sought to deal with her own traumatic experiences. Thus, we see Lengyel name and characterise specific war criminals who were tried at Nuremberg and were wanted for other trials, and to tell the stories of those who did not survive (see Thonfeld). And, as Sheila E. Jelen has argued, Lengyel likely borrowed Dr. Gisella Perl's report of infanticides in Auschwitz to narrate her experience of the murder of her own children on arrival in the camp, to process this loss and to grieve (see Jelen). Lengyel's testimonies display her agency as part of specific 'ecologies of witnessing'.

Morality and Authority

Edit Jeges, in her comparison of Lengyel's memoir and video testimony (Jeges 2015), highlights morality as a key theme that runs through Lengyel's memoir which she sees as linked to her identity as a woman who carries responsibility for her children as well as her parents (Jeges 2015, 238). Lengyel presents herself as a 'reliable witness' in the 'factual tone in her memoir – indeed, hers is considered to be among the most "artless" eyewitness accounts ever published' (Jeges 2015, 237). Such stylistic 'artlessness' of her reportage may also be a deliberate gendered move, Lengyel seeking to avoid questionable emotional tropes often associated with women's writing, such as hysteria and overwrought feelings.

In *Five Chimneys* Lengyel offers a short and concise introduction of her family and social situation at the start; the bulk of her narrative is taken up with the experience of deportation and imprisonment, and the end of the memoir has a short section on liberation and an epilogue in which Lengyel, as mentioned above, clarifies her purpose for writing and affirms her surviving sense of morality and dignity:

> Yet I saw many internees cling to their human dignity to the very end. The Nazis succeeded in degrading them physically, but they could not debase them morally. Because of these few, I have not entirely lost my faith in mankind. (Lengyel 2000, 229)

This 'moral' framing of her memoir tallies with Lengyel's brief description of her upper-middle-class social background (Lengyel 2000, 11–12). Lengyel suggests that she and her family were aware of the persecution and murder of Jews in Nazi-occupied countries including, from 1943, the existence of camps, though she found it hard to 'believe such horrible stories. We still looked upon the Germans as a nation which had given much culture to the world' (Lengyel 2000, 13). Lengyel's narrative in her memoir is devoid of any ethnic or religious markers, even though it is clear from the entire context and other evidence that Lengyel and her family were Jewish (Carmilly-Weinberger 1994, 122, 178). Striking in the early pages of the book is a mobilisation of a cultural affinity with Germany that sits awkwardly alongside the already communicated knowledge of German atrocities during the war and occupation. Lengyel's husband is arrested and stands to be deported to Germany; she suggests that she has the 'option' of accompanying him (Lengyel 2000, 14).[3] And while she anticipates hardship, she presents herself as opting to keep the family together and join the transport, consistent with the role of the dutiful wife and mother (see also Jeges 2015, 237). From this point in her memoir Lengyel maintains that she carried the responsibility for her family's deportation and the murder of her sons and parents and that throughout she upheld the moral standards to which she had been educated, even though she also acknowledges that all actual decisions were really taken by the German occupiers and imprisoners. She cements the image of the dutiful wife and daughter through the narrative of the deportation journey which closes with a dialogue scene where she asks her parents for forgiveness before disembarking the train at Auschwitz. Her parents assure her of having 'always been the best of daughters' and predicting that she has 'the strength to fight, and you will live. You can still do so much for yourself, and the others' (Lengyel 2000, 22). Who the others are becomes clear after the murder of her children, when the narrative turns to accounts of Lengyel's work for the camp resistance and her professional contribution as a prisoner functionary to the running of the infirmary. In encounters with other prisoners, Lengyel presents herself as in charge of directing situations and intervening on behalf of others.

Through such relentless self-assertion, Lengyel maintains her cultural origins and writes herself into a position of moral superiority while emphasising traditional feminine tropes of loyalty, service and care for others, in contrast to overt displays of emotion, lack of (self-) control and unreliable female bodies, also qualities commonly associated with women. This is an effective strategy that ensures that Lengyel's testimony is received and heard. In 1946/47 and in the 1950s, her testimony's publishing history suggests that her account was sought after. While never reaching a huge public audience, among those working on women's testimony and

---

[3] The French memoir presents the decision-making process much more abruptly, without much preface about the context of Lengyel's family's pre-war life, nor is there any suggestion that Lengyel contemplated a possible contribution of her husband to overcome 'a shortage of medical men in Germany'. Rather, the French text charges the German occupiers with deception that led Lengyel to make the decision to accompany her husband (Lengyel 1946, 18f.).

distinctive female experiences of Auschwitz from the mid-1980s onwards, Lengyel's memoir(s) is an established reference point. This suggests that the rediscovery of early testimony in the 'era of the witness' resonated within scholarship that pays particular attention to women and female health care professionals, countering the hitherto male-dominated and universalising approach to the study of testimony.

Religion and Identity

Carmelle Stephens has drawn attention to the religious framing of the memoir, beginning with the opening lines '*Mea culpa*, my fault, *mea maxima culpa!*' (Lengyel 2000, 11) drawn directly from the opening confession of the Catholic mass, and the allusion throughout the narrative to 'the cultural motif of mater dolorosa – "mother of sorrow"' (Stephens 2020, 97). Lengyel thus presents her perceived agency in condemning her sons and mother to death through the trope of the confessing sinner and frames her fate as 'a woman who suffered, lost her husband, parents, children, and friends' (Lengyel 2000, 227) through the image of the mourning Mary, mother of God, in Catholic tradition. Lengyel establishes her sense of self in her memoir in relation to the responsibilities of a wife and mother; in acting in both capacities, she suffers and sees herself as accountable. Stephens argues that Lengyel here projects both maternal virtue through the 'mother of sorrow' figure and offers 'a counter-narrative to the perversion of maternity at Auschwitz' and 'facilitates a symbolic order in a fundamentally disordered universe' (Stephens 2020, 105). Using Catholic religious tropes to communicate with the reader can be read in different ways. On the one hand, it can appeal to the cultural context of her readership that, in the French edition at least, would have been predominantly culturally Catholic. On the other hand, it can also serve to locate Lengyel herself in the cultural context of her youth—she was educated in a Catholic school—and reinforce her social sense of self as part of the Cluj elite, fully assimilated and hardly associated with the ethnically, culturally and religiously Jewish population of her city of birth (Turda 2016, 74–76). Either way, the religious and gendered framing of Lengyel's memoir serves to maintain her narrative and figurative control not over her fate, but over the narration of her experiences, their meaning and the meaning assigned to the decisions she made in spring 1944. Catholic discourse of accountability in Lengyel's memoir also serves to indict the Nazis she sees throughout as ultimately responsible for the fate of her family and her own. These strategies, read with Pollin-Galay's concept 'ecologies of witnessing', suggest that Lengyel responded to her intended post-war readership's cultural frame of reference and, at the same time, maintained her own cultural sense of self in constructing her memoir.

Further evidence for seeing Lengyel's choice of Catholic imagery may be gleaned from her video testimony recorded fifty years after the publication of her memoir. Here Lengyel addresses a different audience, one for whom the Holocaust is cultural knowledge and who has many sources of information about this genocide at their disposal. The interview is framed by the demands of the USC Shoah Foundation's aims and the presence of the interviewer who works through a predefined standard set of questions to shape the survivor's narrative. However, Lengyel chooses how to position herself in this framework and asserts control over her narrative and self-presentation. Jeges reads the video testimony as a way of 'raising public awareness of racism' (Jeges 2015, 236) while also responding to the construction of the eyewitness key to the recording process itself (Jeges 2015, 244). Jeges is interested in the rather different presentation of Lengyel's femininity in the video testimony which communicates a self-assuredness of independent purpose. This points to an opportunity to explore further the ways in which Lengyel seeks to take control of the oral testimony in ways that parallel and enhance her self-presentation in the written account.

CONTROL AND 'EMBELLISHMENT'

Life before deportation takes up 1h23min in the video testimony that is altogether 5hs21min long, and the last 2hs and 21min are about the escape from the death march and the long and convoluted journey to Paris after the war's end. Thus the narrative about deportation and imprisonment in Auschwitz takes up less than 2hs. Lengyel clearly chooses where to place the emphasis, giving elaborate answers to the questions she wishes to dwell on and answering swiftly at other times. She is also not afraid to let the interviewer encounter her silence after a curt reply. For example, when asked whether she married again after the war, Lengyel simply says 'no' and it takes the interviewer 16s of silence to move to the next question (Part II, 56min). Lengyel controls this direct lie which also serves to forestall any questions about a further child she may have had with her second husband.

The video testimony is closest in style to the memoir when Lengyel recounts the experiences of the death march, her and her comrades' escape, liberation and onward journey to France. Here she is consistently in command and the interviewer interjects questions less often, letting Lengyel unfold her own version of her life story where she directs her post-war fate and presents herself in control of her destiny. Lengyel narrates here as she does in her memoir, foregrounding her agency and decision-making. She is self-made even in the post-war world, though accepting the help of her extended family in France, she writes her memoir to inform the world of her experiences and of the dangers that a single 'insane person' can inflict on the world (Part II, 31min). Her life in the United States proceeds by invitation and is built on the success of *Five Chimneys*; her legacy is the Memorial Foundation which continues the charitable legacy of her parents and influences the world (Part II, 1h). Closing her testimony thus comes full circle to the opening of the interview with Nancy Fisher where Lengyel elaborates on her childhood, education and social self-understanding. Asked to state her name and date of birth, Lengyel introduces herself as 'Dr. Olga Lengyel' and gives her birthdate as 19 October 1918, inventing the doctorate and making herself 10 years younger. The description of her childhood home focuses on being Hungarian—Cluj is always Kolozsvár, her native language is Hungarian, her family is rooted in this city and part of its social elite as her father is an entrepreneur and her mother heads charitable foundations, notably an orphanage. While Lengyel's husband is mentioned, she emerges here more strongly as an upper-middle-class daughter of a well-established family; her education is cosmopolitan European with governesses from Germany, France and England, at the Catholic grammar school for girls, and completed with a degree in literature. Her family is invested in character, that is who one is morally is important—a bridge to her memoir—rather than assigning any importance to ethnic or religious origins. Lengyel deflects and counters questions about religion, describing herself as not brought up religious, but with an emphasis on culture and being at home in a multi-ethnic and multi-religious society, religion 'is such a private question' (Part I, 21min). Asked whether her family belonged to a synagogue and observed the holidays, Lengyel is evasive, confirming her Jewish origins but aligning herself with the intellectual elite of Kolozsvár. She also sounds annoyed at this point that the interviewer belabours questions of religion and ethnicity. This does not interest Lengyel. Rather, she insists on establishing herself in her audience's mind as a cosmopolitan upper-middle-class European woman, and she maintains this posture throughout the interview. Astonishingly and in contrast to the memoir where she suggests that she had known about German atrocities, even though she had trouble believing them, in the video testimony Lengyel devotes much time to praising German culture. She claims that while she had heard rumours about gas vans, she attributed these to anti-German British propaganda and dismissed them (Part I, 1h21min).

Where embellishment and invention serve to establish Lengyel's authority and consistent morality in the memoir, dwelling on pre-deportation life and her cosmopolitan social self-understanding take on a similar function in the video testimony. Throughout, Lengyel is concerned to present herself as coherent in personality, in social status and in belonging. The video testimony's visual setup reinforces this self-image. Lengyel is positioned in the European-style interior of her New York home, dressed exquisitely and maintaining her poise throughout the interview (see also Jeges 2015, 245). She embodies what she relates in regard to her social and cultural origins and thereby her video testimony confirms in a different way the aims of her memoir—the projection of a consistent identity in charge of her own destiny.

Filmed fifty years after the publication of her memoir, the video testimony speaks and is released into a radically altered cultural context. Lengyel's heavily accented English, her poise and the environment of filming create a different relationship with her audience than her book(s). In this new 'ecology', Lengyel has the opportunity to connect with an audience that has easy access to historical information about Auschwitz, while being far less sure about the details of Hungarian Jewish life, the aftermath of the camps and the chaos of liberation. This new setting may account for her dwelling on her early childhood and youth along with a far longer narrative of her experiences since leaving Birkenau on a death march. At the same time, her advanced age also suggests that Lengyel's video testimony responds to her own need to speak of her family and, in a sense, memorialise them on camera, aware that there is nobody else able to conjure an image of her childhood in Kolozsvár. Hence, Lengyel responds to two contexts of witnessing at the same time, her own and that of her audience. She has to hold them in parallel and respond to her interviewer who consistently seeks to interrupt the focus on Lengyel's childhood and youth, in order to move to what she, Nancy Fisher, considers the most significant part of the interview, that is deportation and imprisonment.

With the overall parameters of comparison between written and oral testimony clarified, the remainder of this chapter focuses on three episodes that are represented differently in Lengyel's memoir(s) and in her USC Shoah Foundation video testimony. I will demonstrate that we can observe the changing relationships of Lengyel to the shape of her own experiences and trace the evolution of wider society's engagement with survivor testimony: in the opening of her testimony and her deportation report; in Lengyel's narrative of resistance activity in the camp and in the post-war narrative of her experiences of a death march, liberation and onward journey to Paris.

Deportation

The opening of Lengyel's testimony and the narrative of her family's deportation from Cluj to Auschwitz-Birkenau in May 1944 establish Lengyel as a narrator to her readers and listeners. Here she positions herself in relation to her family and culture of origin.[4]

Comparing the French and English memoirs, it is notable that the opening sections of the French version are much shorter than in the English. The French edition gives hardly any reference to pre-war life, other than that Lengyel's husband was a distinguished doctor and that she was assisting him and also had some medical training. The wider family is not introduced, the two sons are mentioned, but without any details or names. The English version includes inner monologues seeking to detail Lengyel's thought processes interpreting the events and introduces her sons by name. The narrative is increasingly dramatised with additional dialogues and lengthening of scenes that in the French are simply directly reported. For example, the French version reports the mounting deaths in the cattle car during the deportation from Cluj to Auschwitz-Birkenau matter-of-factly and with compassion (Lengyel 1946, 24–25), while the

---

[4] In regard to all three episodes considered in this chapter, there are no relevant differences in the narrative between the English editions. Therefore, the discussion will work with the Academy Chicago Publishers edition and compare that to the French publication from 1946 and to the USC Shoah Foundation testimony from 1998. The deportation narrative can be found on pages 17-46 of *Souvenirs de l'au-delà* (Lengyel 1946) and pages 11-31 of the most recent English edition (Lengyel 2000); in the USC Shoah Foundation testimony, Lengyel speaks about the deportation from 1:02-1:57hs in Part I.

English version dramatises with insertions such as 'Death in the car! A gasp of horror ran through the tightly packed mass of humans. [...] "We have a corpse in our midst. My father has died." "Keep your corpse, [...] You will have many more of them soon!"' (Lengyel 2000, 19). The prevalence of dramatisation in the English text may point to the new publication context. While the French version is directed at the immediate post-war audience in Europe with the purpose of amassing evidence of the genocide of Jews in Europe and reflecting on the prosecution of war criminals, the English edition is aimed towards an American readership. Here, dissemination of information is still a relevant aim, but prosecution of war criminals is of lesser significance in 1947 America.

In the video testimony, the narrative of the deportation is prefaced by an extensive section on Lengyel's pre-war life as detailed above. In Part I, 1h02min, Lengyel moves to detail her family's deportation with 'our family tragedy really started in 38/39'. She reveals more details about how she understands her husband's summon to the Gestapo that preceded deportation: he was denounced (and expropriated) by a new colleague, Dr. Auswald or Osvald, who she describes as a charitable hire by Dr. Lengyel as Auswald/Osvald had a large family and needed additional income. Auswald/Osvald, Lengyel alleges, was really a collaborator with the Nazi occupiers and had informed on her husband's boycott of German pharmaceutical companies. The focus of the interview with the USC Shoah Foundation includes much personal reflection on the experience of denunciation and loss of faith in the cultural certainties of her youth, that is, Lengyel's painful and thorough disillusionment with German culture and Germans. The need to comment on the destruction of German culture and her trust in Germans runs as a thread through the video testimony, even to the point of seeking confirmation about the existence and purpose of gas chambers from an 'Aryan German' inmate in Birkenau (Part I, 1h65min).

In other respects, the narrative in the USC Shoah Foundation interview repeats episodes reported in the French and English memoirs. Thus, Lengyel retells the story of the wife of a colleague attempting suicide during deportation in the cattle car, her husband pumping her stomach and the last conversation with her parents before disembarking at Auschwitz. She mentions the extraordinariness of the scenes on the eight-day transport, with people dying and others singing the prayer for the dead.[5] The account of the selection is less detailed in the video testimony. She describes briefly how both her children were selected for death together, that she placed her father in a waiting ambulance and that she asked whether her mother could accompany the children. She frames this account again as part of her being deceived by the Germans, while, at the same time, she cannot and does not want 'to liberate' herself from the 'fact' that she condemned her family to death (Part I, 1h33min): she acted to protect them and was wrong because she trusted the Germans (Part I, 1h34min). Since that moment, Lengyel says, she has suffered from nightly insomnia, being haunted by the image of her mother and children being led away. Lengyel is prompted to show her tattooed number—25,403 (Part I, 1h53min), and relates that even though she had been offered repeatedly to get the tattoo removed, 'this would be a big mistake, because this is what I am' (Part I, 1h54min). Lengyel appears to narrate more personal detail in the video testimony, while remaining faithful to the instances reported in her memoirs, framing her entire account until this point in relation to her slow and repeated disillusionment with everything German. She appears here to respond to two needs of witnessing at the same time: the need to account for her relationship to German culture and the need to include testimonial tropes recognisable to her American audience, such as the selection on arrival, the tattooing and the insistence of contemporary audiences to inscribe survivors with an identity that remains forever tied to their imprisonment.

Even more pronouncedly, the section about arrival in Auschwitz also seems to respond to audience expectations in the United States in the late 1990s. Lengyel arrived in May 1944 in Auschwitz, when the railway ramp in Birkenau may not yet have been operational (see Rudorff 2018, 16:20). Indeed, Lengyel mentions that she arrived near Auschwitz I and saw the gate spelling 'Arbeit macht frei', before being driven to Birkenau (Part I, 1h35min). Her description of the shower on arrival in Birkenau is interspersed with reference to the possibility of gas rather than water being dispensed (Part I, 1h38min), which sounds more like a retrospective because the memoirs and the interview locate the awareness of gas

---

[5] While Lengyel hardly ever mentions religion and does not identify herself as ethnically or religiously Jewish in her memoirs and does so only when pressed in the video testimony, subtle hints such as the reference to the 'mourner's chant' (*Kaddish*) in both the French and English versions, identify the deportees, and thus herself, as Jewish (Lengyel 1946, 24f.; 2000, 19).

chambers and mass murder days after arrival in Auschwitz. Such instances along with the image of the crematoria where flames are shooting out of the chimneys as a fellow inmate informs her that 'this is where your family is', suggest an awareness of the American audience of the USC Shoah Foundation testimony. This audience may have expectations about what arrival at Auschwitz should look like, and may, therefore, be expecting references to showers, gas and crematoria in a specific 'Spielberg-esque' or Hollywood-dramatised manner.

A similar strategy of responding to perceived audience expectations and to project a sense of control over both the narrative and the events that are narrated is detectable in Lengyel's account of her involvement with the camp resistance in Birkenau. These concerns do not always complement each other easily, but also reveal the tension between the projection of a public image of herself in control and in full knowledge of the extent of the crimes committed by Nazi Germany, and the challenge of processing a complicated relationship with her own powerlessness.

Resistance

Lengyel's narrative of resistance activity in the camp is among the most embellished sections of her memoir and relies on the amalgamation of the experiences of a number of different people. In her video testimony these sequences are relatively quickly told.[6] Placing these sections next to each other, it becomes clear that her written and oral testimonies of resistance work relate to Lengyel's public persona as a Holocaust survivor, and that they fulfil different functions in 1946/47 and 1998. In the memoirs, Lengyel's narrative of activities in the camp resistance establishes her authority as narrator and witness and bolsters her social position as part of the Cluj elite, not least her ability to relate to SS Dr. Klein. In the video testimony, her social status is established visually through the filming taking place in a European-style bourgeois interior and through her pre-war narrative about her family and education. In 1998 Lengyel omits an embellished and synthesising narrative of the experiences and actions of her inmate cohort. The facts of these episodes are well-established and Lengyel does not need to reference them, nor can she credibly claim more authority and activity in the camp than she actually had.

---

[6] Key passages in the French memoir are pages 113-33 and 251-261, and pages 78-89 and 167-176 in English, Part I, 1h57min-2h23min.

Lengyel narrates her initiation into the camp resistance in both memoirs without significant differences. The person, 'L.', recruiting her is giving her a reason to live when she felt suicidal and tasks her with three things: to disseminate news to boost the morale of inmates, to act as a 'post office' for correspondence and to remember everything she sees in the camp to be able to tell the world the truth after the war (Lengyel 1946, 115–16; 2000, 80–81). These tasks give Lengyel a reason to live (Lengyel 1946, 116; 2000, 81). She closes the section on resistance in English with an additional paragraph missing in French:

> I had then two reasons to live: one, to work with the resistance movement and help as long as I could stand upon my feet; two to dream and pray for the day to come when I could go free and tell the world, 'This is what I saw with my own eyes. It must never be allowed to happen again!' (Lengyel 2000, 89)

Lengyel thus reinforces the framing of her memoir for her American audience as imbued with a mission to resist the genocide and to tell the world. She adds the slogan 'never again' which, in this context, originated with survivors of Buchenwald concentration camp (Popescu and Schult 2020, 135), and, by the late 1940s, was finding resonance in Israel and the United States.

In the USC Shoah Foundation testimony, Lengyel does not foreground a concern with the time after the war, but focuses on her agency in controlling her fate. She states that she did not want to be controlled by the Germans (Part I, 1h59min) and, in her depression, wanted to choose the manner of her death by walking into the electrified fence surrounding Birkenau. Here, she alleges, she was pulled back by 'the head of the French resistance', naming him as Maurice Lequeux (Part I, 2h56min). Lengyel gives more details of the resistance activities she claims to have been involved in, particularly the smuggling of explosives hidden in a vegetable patch outwith the camp, via the Jewish women's camp infirmary where she worked, and on to the *Sonderkommando* (Part I, 1h15min). Aspects of this narrative are covered much later in the memoirs: a chapter entitled 'Résistance' (251–256) and following (257–261), and 'The Underground' (167–176) which detail the smuggling of explosives with Lengyel alleging that she was involved in handling packages but without detail about their origins.

The video testimony frames the resistance narrative in relation to the war and encouraging news about the progress of the Allies. Lengyel appears keen to understand the resistance activities in Auschwitz as part of a larger strategy to defeat Nazi Germany and to suggest to the listener that inmates were in touch with current affairs in the outside world. Such framing is absent in the memoirs where the focus is directly on the events in the camp and Lengyel being active in collecting information for dissemination in the post-war world. In 1998, she no longer needs to perform the latter task, but instead appears more concerned to show her own agency in interpreting and engaging directly with the progress of the war even from within Auschwitz-Birkenau death camp.

Until the end of imprisonment, Lengyel's narrative strategies across memoirs and video testimony are consistent with her need to preserve narrative control over her life and to relate her fate in ways that resonate with the audiences she envisages. This somewhat changes in relation to the episodes following her escape from a death march.

LIBERATION

The ending of the French memoir differs considerably from the ending of the English version, and the 1998 testimony, while preserving the broad outlines of the ending of the English memoir, covers a much more convoluted narrative that is challenging to listen to. The French version ends with three short chapters, the first of which 'L'Amour à l'Ombre du Krematorium' has a counterpart in the English edition, however, the English narrative is much embellished and focuses on the alleged sexual depravity of SS guard Irma Grese. The final chapter's account of the torture of children in the infirmary is folded into the post-script to the English edition which also includes reflections on how readers may be able to use the information related in the memoir to spur them on to prevent future genocides. The French book ends with Lengyel departing the camp on a death march. The penultimate chapters of the English book following 'Love in the shadow of the crematory' address her search for her husband ('In the death car'), followed by two chapters on the death march and liberation ('On the threshold of the unknown', 'Freedom').

The neat endings of both written memoirs are not mirrored in the video testimony. Here, the narrative beginning in Part I, 3h06min continues until Part II, 21min when she begins her stay with her cousin,

László Légman, in Paris to recover and then write her book. Consistent with the narrative in the memoir is Lengyel's insistence throughout on controlling the direction her life takes from the escape from the death march onwards. In Part I, 3h31min she names the Polish man whose family saved her and her two companions as Ludwik Paszek, a former mayor of the Polish village who sheltered them for three weeks in January–February 1945 (https://collections.yadvashem.org/en/righteous/4039766), but does not remember the other couple she named in the Yad Vashem file honouring rescuers of Jews as 'righteous among the nations', Augustyn and Zofia Godziek. Throughout this narrative Lengyel is very animated, gesticulating a lot for emphasis. The journey from liberation in a Polish village to her arrival in France in March 1945 is convoluted and peppered with references to the command of the French underground during the war and various alleged tensions between the British and French Allied commands. None of this is present in the memoirs, which end with the death march (French) and liberation in a Polish village (English). The liberation narrative in the English book concludes with the arrival of the Russian army:

> Now we heard a new language, a language foreign to us, and saw people we had never seen before; but they had brought us the greatest gift that life can give – liberty! (Lengyel 2000, 223)

The video testimony qualifies this somewhat. In Part I, 3h37min Lengyel suggests that she was awoken one night by Russian soldiers who were searching the house she was staying in for Germans. She explains that these soldiers were 'not the real Russian army', but a cohort of ex-convicts sent to search the area before the arrival of the actual Russian army (see also Jeges 2015, 250). One of these soldiers pulls her up and wants to drag her outside, tearing her clothes, pushing her to the floor and ripping her watch off her arm with his teeth (Part I, 3h40min). The narrative suggests that she was raped. Lengyel continues that she decided not to report the assault to the Russian army command, but that she asks to leave, in order to return to 'her children at home', which is granted (Part I, 3h45min). It is possible that this is the first time that Lengyel has voiced this experience at the end of the war, consistent with many women not reporting rape at the time and later having difficulty naming the experience. What is striking, however, is that even in this narrative of humiliation and brutalisation, Lengyel presents herself as in charge of the outcome, namely that she is able to leave under the pretence of wishing to return home to her (dead) children.

Throughout the video testimony, it is notable that Lengyel relates very quickly and without much detail many very traumatic experiences she had reported at greater length in her memoirs: the selection of her children for death and the infanticides she witnessed and participated in. The rape by a Russian soldier, on the other hand, is introduced for the first time, and she carefully ensures that the traumatic narrative does not unseat the image of the Russian army as liberators (he was not part of the 'real Russian army, but a former convict') and thereby located within her own moral universe. The scene takes a couple of minutes to relate and there is a lot of circumstantial detail about how she was dragged and groped, the rape itself encapsulated in the theft of her watch (a gift from her rescuers), an item of value and a symbol of her virtue which is violently snatched. Lengyel also folds the trauma of the murder of her children into the trauma of the post-war sexual assault, creating a narrative parallel that underlines the lasting significance of the experience.

There are several possibilities for interpreting this narrative sequence. In relation to Lengyel's testimonies operating in specific 'ecologies of witnessing', we can read the account of sexual violence as a response to the late 1990s focus on women's experiences during the Holocaust that created the possibility for women survivors to articulate their specifically female traumatisation. Hence it is possible here to stipulate a coincidence between Lengyel's need to verbalise her experience of sexual violence and the context of witnessing that enabled this testimony to be recorded.

CONCLUSION

What historiographical gain may arise from this close, comparative reading of Lengyel's written and oral testimonies? While we learn no new facts from Lengyel and, acknowledging Langer's concerns (Langer 2021), need to be extremely cautious about her embellishments verging on outright falsehoods, I would suggest that there is still a lot that can be learned from such engagement.

Firstly, by placing three versions of her testimony next to each other, we have been able to observe how Lengyel sought to engage her audience situated in different 'ecologies' that enable particular forms of witnessing. In 1946 France, the need to communicate directly and authoritatively to establish the genocide of Jews in Europe in the minds of a wider public was acute. Lengyel chooses modes of presentation that address this need: she is an eyewitness survivor and she can supply details of what went on in Auschwitz and what she and others experienced, including statistics. This, and her impeccably bourgeois morality and social class lend her authority (Jeges 2015, 237 establishes this in relation to the English text). The English version of 1947 reinforces this portrait and extends it to an American audience with further embellishment. In 1998, the ninety-year-old Lengyel revisits her testimony and is filmed for the USC Shoah Foundation, working along a prescribed tripartite structure of before the Holocaust-during-after, so that Lengyel has the opportunity to expand on her upbringing and pre-deportation cultural identity. As Jeges has noted, the visual setup of the testimony adds further observable detail to the class background Lengyel describes (Jeges 2015, 44–46). The changed format and different cultural context establish Lengyel's authority visually and largely dispense with the moralising tone of the memoirs, and she takes charge of her narrative often in spite of her interviewer. Lengyel furthers her authoritative voice by interpreting her war-time decisions frequently in relation to world events such as the progress of the Allies and the work of the French national resistance. This models to her American audience cultural competence in relating personal experience to pressing concerns of the day, suggesting to her listeners that their own social and political engagement matters.

Secondly, we can trace scholarly concerns with survivor testimony across the decades. Lengyel's testimonies have been interpreted repeatedly, not least as part of a corpus of early Holocaust testimonies by women that enabled the introduction of gender-specific analyses of victim experiences. Along with Gisella Perl and others, Lengyel carved out a format of relating what she wanted to say about her experiences of deportation, incarceration, slave labour and liberation, including sexual violence, medical experiments and infanticide. Lengyel was part of birthing a new genre and verbalising gender-based experiences of atrocity frankly, but in ways designed to connect with her audience (such as her own traditional femininity and morality in the memoirs, and the verbalisation of her own rape in the 1998 video testimony). Today, Lengyel's testimonies offer an opportunity for scholars to interrogate our own blindspots and limitations in interpreting testimony.

Finally, all her testimonies are consistent in the main—embellished— episodes that are reported, including evident falsehoods and inventions, while the video testimony adds more, and plausible, personal details.

Carrying the same stories with her, from the first publication to her final testimony, indicates that these stories *are* her and that we cannot distinguish the survivor from the embellishment of their story. What we can do is engage repeatedly with Lengyel's testimonial statements and actualise them in the new contexts in which we hear them. Thereby we add successive 'ecologies' of engagement that each carry the opportunity to extend our understanding of this particular survivor's voice.

References

Carmilly-Weinberger, Moshe. 1994. *The Road to Life: The Rescue Operation of Jewish Refugees on the Hungarian-Romanian Border in Transylvania, 1936–1944.* New York: Shengold.

Jeges, Edit. 2015. 'Gendering the Cultural Memory of the Holocaust: A Comparative Analysis of a Memoir and a Video Testimony by Olga Lengyel'. In *Women and the Holocaust*, edited by Andrea Pető, Louise Hecht, and Karolina Krasuska, 233–53. Central European University Press. https://doi.org/10.7829/j.ctt1t6p69c.

Langer, Lawrence. 2021. Memory and Invention in Olga Lengyel's Five Chimneys. In *The Afterdeath of the Holocaust*, ed. Lawrence Langer, 169–195. Cham: Springer International Publishing. https://doi.org/10.1007/978-3-030-66139-7_9.

Lengyel, Olga. 1946. *Souvenirs de l'au-delà*. Translated by Ladislas Gara. Paris: Éditions du Bateau Ivre.

Lengyel, Olga. 1985. *Five Chimneys: A Woman Survivors True Story of Auschwitz.* Reprint of 1947 edition by Ziff Davis Publishing Co. London: Granada Publishing.

Lengyel, Olga. 2000. *Five Chimneys: A Woman Survivor's True Story of Auschwitz.* Chicago, IL: Academy Chicago Publ.

Pollin-Galay, Hannah. 2019. *Ecologies of Witnessing: Language, Place, and Holocaust Testimony.* New Haven: Yale University Press.

Popescu, Diana I., and Tanja Schult. 2020. Performative Holocaust Commemoration in the 21st Century. *Holocaust Studies* 26 (2): 135–151. https://doi.org/10.1080/17504902.2019.1578452.

Rudorff, Andrea, ed. 2018. *Das KZ Auschwitz 1942–1945 und die Zeit der Todesmärsche 1944/45.* Vol. 16. Die Verfolgung und Ermordung der europäischen Juden durch das nationalsozialistische Deutschland 1933–1945. De Gruyter. https://doi.org/10.1515/9783110573787.

Stephens, Carmelle. 2020. Saints and Martyrs: Popular Maternal Tropes in Holocaust Memoir. *The Journal of Holocaust Research* 34 (2): 95–110. https://doi.org/10.1080/25785648.2020.1741847.

Turda, Marius. 2016. Redemptive Family Narratives: Olga Lengyel and the Textuality of the Holocaust. *Archiva Moldaviae* 8: 69–82.

WEBSITES (LAST ACCESSED JUNE 2024)

https://collections.yadvashem.org/en/righteous/4039766

CHAPTER 5

Morality Turned Upside Down: Perpetrators in the Eyes of Olga Lengyel

Christoph Thonfeld

Abstract Olga Lengyel's experiences as an inmate of Auschwitz-Birkenau fundamentally challenged her idea of a moral order with the enforced insight that perpetrators can be beautiful people who do evil things. Throughout her narrative, she is rather focused on how she perceives perpetrators' behaviour in the camp and what meaning she can assign to their moral conduct and outer appearance. Mainly in the English version of her 1946/47 book, she designed roles for them to play in her attempt to recreate her own moral universe in the aftermath of World War II by integrating her experience of Auschwitz-Birkenau into it. In her 1998 interview for the USC Shoah Foundation, however, she was mainly concerned with her personal legacy. Olga Lengyel's two main testimonies are examined within a synopsis of accounts by fellow survivors in an attempt to bring the study of multiple testimonies of survivors together with perpetrator research. What follows is an investigation of the functions of representations of perpetrators in Lengyel's and others' accounts, with special attention on the question of how survivors' testimonies and media coverage shaped the public perception of Nazi perpetrators in the post-war years.

Keywords Morality · Beauty · Perpetrators · Order

© The Author(s), under exclusive license to Springer Nature
Switzerland AG 2025
P. Davies et al., *Olga Lengyel, Auschwitz Survivor*,
https://doi.org/10.1007/978-3-031-82490-6_5

103

INTRODUCTION

In an article fundamentally challenging the veracity of Olga Lengyel's *Five Chimneys*, the English version of her memoir originally published in 1947, Lawrence Langer attacks his fellow literary scholar Tzvetan Todorov's positive take on the possibility of moral behaviour of prisoners in concentration camps (Todorov 1997). For Langer, this inevitably leads to a misrepresentation of the reality of Auschwitz. The moral conduct of human beings in Auschwitz had also been Lengyel's main measure to assess her own and others' actions and interactions in the camp. In Langer's view, 'Todorov uses Lengyel to support his thesis that moral life could flourish in a German concentration camp' (Langer 2021, 171). Consequently, Langer also questions Lengyel's discursive framing of her reflections on her experiences at Auschwitz-Birkenau as a moral challenge to be overcome. However, instead of dismissing Lengyel's standpoint as presumptuous, it deserves to be taken seriously to find out what it tells us about Olga Lengyel's ways of dealing with her memories of Auschwitz and what impact they have had on her biographical trajectory.

A core issue for Lengyel, as I will argue, was to put her capacity to act as a moral human being on trial. With the opening phrase of *Five Chimneys*, 'I cannot acquit myself of the charge that I am, in part, responsible for the destruction of my own parents and of my two young sons' (Lengyel 2000, 11), she invokes a courtroom setting, casting herself in the role of prosecutor and defendant at the same time. She sounds less dramatic and more oriented towards what she refers to as facts, though, in the 1946 French version of her book *Souvenirs de l'au-delà*, stating 'Je me sens responsable de la mort de mes parents et mes deux fils. Voici les faits' (Lengyel 1946, 17). However, the judicial character of the language is likely not only an effect of the English translation. On the whole, the English text adds or expands aspects and perspectives that were not articulated at all or were articulated far less explicitly in the French edition. Additionally, Lengyel's narration in *Five Chimneys* suggests that her memories were overshadowed by a feeling of survivor guilt, as she concludes her opening phrase with the emphatic claim 'that I could have, I might have, saved them'.

Lengyel's experiences as an inmate of Auschwitz-Birkenau fundamentally challenged her idea of a moral order when she learned, through observation, that perpetrators can be beautiful people who do evil things (Lengyel 2000, 50). Throughout her narrative, she focuses on how she perceives perpetrators' behaviour in the camp and what meaning she can assign to their moral conduct and outer appearance, but less on what they actually did to her personally. Mainly in the English version of the book, perpetrators are, thus, not chiefly presented as sources of her own misery. Rather, she designs roles for them to play in her attempt to recreate her own moral universe in the aftermath of World War II by integrating her experience of Auschwitz-Birkenau into it. As far as Lengyel's interactions with well-known perpetrators at Auschwitz-Birkenau are concerned, Langer ties Lengyel's 'emphasis ... on her ability to establish bonds with vicious camp functionaries like Dr Fritz Klein and Irma Grese' to her ambition to claim 'that even in Auschwitz one could remain a partial agent of one's own fate' (Langer 2021, 194–195). As Hannah Holtschneider argues in her chapter in this book, reclaiming agency was one of Olga Lengyel's main objectives in writing down her memories.

She penned her memoir soon after liberation while trying to recover from the harrowing experiences she had between the spring of 1944 and January 1945. When she was working on the manuscript in the latter half of 1945 and early 1946 in Paris, where she had arrived after a winding route through war-torn Eastern Europe, she was basically at the same stage of her life that she had been in when she was sent to Auschwitz. A Jewish woman in her late thirties, of Transylvanian origin with an assimilated Hungarian social background, there were barely any intermittent layers of experience that would have changed her view of her memories. However, the encounters Lengyel had with former fellow inmates during the death march after leaving Auschwitz and during her period of rehabilitation must have shaped her memories to some extent. By her own account, for example, she shared some part of her escape route with her former fellow medical orderly from the Jewish women's infirmary in Birkenau's camp B II c, Lujza Salamon (Rudorff 2020, 9–10). And during her journey through Poland after liberation, she allegedly again encountered Maurice Lequeux, a French resistance fighter, someone who is supposed to have been with her at Auschwitz. They were reported to have met in early March 1945 at an Allied diplomat's office in Lublin.[1]

---

[1] There are no known records of Olga Lengyel's incarceration in Auschwitz-Birkenau, which happens to be the case for many Jewish deportees at that late stage of extermination operations. After her survival and arrival in Lublin in late February/early March 1945, she again met her French former fellow inmate Maurice Lequeux, who would officially testify there to Lengyel's presence in Birkenau. A report on these events, written by the

Later, in Paris, she met members of her extended family and potentially also Gisella Perl, another fellow Birkenau survivor. Early accounts of survivors, such as Olga Lengyel's *Five Chimneys*, were written without a framework of established scholarly research into the murder of the Jews of Europe and with no existing canon of what is now understood as survivor testimony and Holocaust literature. These accounts became elements of an evolving discourse. Survivors were struggling to find words to express what they had been through with no recognised genre to refer to. Language that today would be deemed offensive or discriminatory had not yet been discursively evaluated, moderated or removed by authors, editors or publisher readers. That eventually resulted in the creation of what Peter Davies calls 'a specific genre of autobiography' in his chapter in this book.

In 1998, when Lengyel gave the USC Shoah Foundation an interview, she did so in a completely different individual, social and historical situation than that which she had been in when she wrote her memoir in 1946. There, she refers back to the circumstances of working on the French edition of her book: 'Paris was dark' (Part II, 0h30min) and says that she suffered from constant nightmares. However, after more than fifty years of living with memories of the experience of life-threatening Nazi persecution, she could now look back on a successful post-war career as a philanthropist educational entrepreneur; her Memorial Library and Art Collection of the Second World War had by that time been turned into The Olga Lengyel Institute for Holocaust Studies and Human Rights in New York. Her position as an established agent in the fields of art and education led to a strong shift in the emphasis of the interview, with her life before and after Auschwitz being more the centre of attention. In particular, Lengyel focused on her departure from Birkenau, the ensuing death march and her escape from it. In her description, she gave several examples of being guided by altruistic motives (she mentioned a number of incidents where she tried to help other inmates) and of overcoming hatred against her former tormentors (as proof, she explained how she helped a Polish acquaintance even after she had found out that he had collaborated with the Nazis). In 1945–47, she had been asking

New Zealander Allied diplomatic envoy Desmond Patrick Costello and filed by the British Special Operations Executive is currently only publicly available in James McNeish, 2008, *The Sixth Man: The Extraordinary Life of Paddy Costello*, London: Quartet Books, where there are quotes from the report referring to Lengyel.

herself troubling questions about her own role in the Auschwitz prisoner hierarchy and, thus, about any possible complicity with the Nazis.
Her ensuing biographical trajectory can be seen as her attempt to give
an emphatic answer to those questions. In 1998, though, she appeared
mainly concerned with her personal legacy and tried to use the interview
to aim for her crowning final achievement by bestowing her literary and
institutional estate on the USC Shoah Foundation (Part II, 1h16min).

Apart from providing case studies for issues surrounding veracity,
biographical accounts also open windows into the analysis of individual perception and interpretation of historic events. In this chapter,
Olga Lengyel's two main testimonies are examined within a synopsis
of accounts by fellow survivors who wrote or talked about their experiences in public or in court immediately after the war, in the 1960s
and/or around the millennium. All these materials are analysed in an
attempt to bring the study of multiple testimonies of survivors together
with perpetrator research. What follows is an investigation of the functions of representations of perpetrators in Olga Lengyel's accounts, with
a focus on the question of how survivors' testimonies and media coverage
shaped the public perception of Nazi perpetrators in the post-war years.
I will show how survivors in their attempts to express their experiences
were influenced by contemporary discourses while at the same time also
feeding into them, and how they tried to come to grips with what Nazi
perpetrators had inflicted on them and what impact this has had on their
personalities and worldviews.

Olga Lengyel's case helps us situate her memoir's position in the
intertextual network of a developing discourse on Nazi perpetrators.
This discourse was only beginning to come into existence when Lengyel
wrote the French and English versions of her book and it had become
much more differentiated and nuanced at the time of her Shoah Foundation interview. However, at the time of writing the first published
versions of her book, her engagement with well-known Nazi perpetrators at Auschwitz seems to have had much more relevance for her than
in the 1998 interview. This leads to the assumption that it was not
so much any concrete experiences with them that she wanted to tell
or any lasting impressions they had made on her that she wanted to
convey. It rather looks like she had considered them helpful in her process
of personal meaning-making in the late 1940s. In the late 1990s, her
biographical account had distinctly lost that focus. In light of this, it
seems worthwhile to investigate how Lengyel's presentation fed into and

was influenced in each case by contemporary views and understandings of Nazi perpetrators.

MEMORIES, MORALS AND PERPETRATION

In the wake of the first Nuremberg trial in 1945/46, perpetrators were mostly assumed to have been members of the SS. Together with the Gestapo, the Security Service of the SS (SD) and the Corps of Political Leaders of the NSDAP, it had been classified as a criminal organisation. The SS as an institution was no longer accepted as part of the sphere of normal life in post-war public opinion across occupied Germany. This was due to the fact that the SS became closely associated with the responsibility for mass crimes: '[W]hile not every SS man was regarded as a killer – ... – every killer had to be an SS man' (Matthäus 2005, 199). This constellation turned out to be a convenient way for members of West German society at large to draw a clear line between themselves and those who had committed the worst atrocities during World War II. The SS became 'the alibi of a nation' (Reitlinger 1981).[2] The process of demonising perpetrators and firmly situating them within the SS was enhanced by West German courts' rejection of the Anglo-American legal concept of 'Common Design'. In this legal concept used by the Allies, the operation of a concentration camp was considered a criminal act and put at the centre of the prosecution before it came to ascribing responsibility for individual crimes. Thus, it made any participation in this operation a criminal act. On the contrary, West German courts based their judgements on the criminal code's understanding of individually and wilfully committing offences with responsibility depending on whether an individual had appropriated an action as his or her own. In order to distance themselves from any wrongdoing, many of the accused claimed that they had acted under superior orders or under (putative) duress. Thus, only 'excess actions' where someone went beyond explicit orders out of one's own initiative could be held liable. Therefore, the courts ended up specifically targeting alleged sadists and perverts, who were the only ones considered wilfully capable of such acts.

---

[2] The 1957 German edition had the dramatically exculpating title, *Die S.S.—Tragödie einer deutschen Epoche*, München: Desch.

Eugen Kogon's 1946 book *Der SS-Staat* (Kogon 2023)[3] was the first attempt to comprehensively describe the inner world of concentration camps and has had a strong impact on the societal perception of and further research into Nazi perpetrators in Germany and abroad. As a sociologist and political scientist who survived Buchenwald, Kogon portrayed SS men predominantly as socially declassed people who utilised power and violence to raise their status and prove their masculinity. While this holds true for numerous concentration camp guards in the early 1930s within Germany, it is also misleading with regard to senior staff and the vast majority of those involved in the mass killings in Eastern Europe during World War II. The division of the Nazi past into a sphere of criminality and one of normality had been successfully established in the West German public in the early 1950s. Historian Frank Bajohr, thus, concluded that popular perception of that past had become structured according to the opposition between 'beasts' and 'zones of decency' (Becker 2009).

In 1945/46, Nazi crimes trials and media coverage of those trials dominated popular perceptions and debate about those actively involved in committing atrocities. Olga Lengyel extensively watched reports on the British Bergen-Belsen trial (Lüneburg/Germany, 17 September to 17 November 1945). She refers to her reception of trial coverage several times in the English edition of her book (Lengyel 2000, 24, 153 and 162) and, with the rare and thus prominent use of a footnote, conveys her view of Fritz Klein, the 'Chief Selector', in her own terminology as 'one of the main attractions' at the Belsen trial. At the same time, survivors across Europe and beyond were trying to come to terms with their ordeal, finding words and making sense of what had happened to them. Lengyel, as one of them, struggled to maintain her self-perception as a moral agent, which she felt had been deeply compromised during her imprisonment in Auschwitz-Birkenau. Foremost in the English version of her memoir, she questioned herself from a moral perspective, based on the idea of being tried in court. Her moral views of society in Hungarian-speaking elite circles in interwar Transylvania which was transferred back from Romania to Hungary in 1940 and her broader worldview had been deeply shaken by the experience of deportation and imprisonment in Auschwitz.

---

[3] A French translation under the title *L'Etat SS* was published in 1947, in English it was published under the title *The Theory and Practice of Hell* in 1950.

Lengyel was clearly still struggling with this for some time after liberation. So many of the individual portraits of people and memories she talks about in the English version of her book are structured by attempts to uphold educated middle-class morals. For the entire duration of her incarceration in Auschwitz-Birkenau, she put herself under intense moral scrutiny ('Our hour of shame had begun', Lengyel 2000, 26), based on her self-perception as a woman who is very conscious of her social status. This shines through in the way she describes observations allegedly made in Birkenau as well, for example, when she laments the 'painful sight' of seeing a 'fine woman' drink from a puddle (Lengyel 2000, 39).

In 1998, Lengyel's social positioning was markedly different from that of 1946/7. From the way she presents herself in the Shoah Foundation interview, her renewed self-assured sense of social status becomes clear, which allows her to bring her own private trial to its conclusion. Emotionally, though, the moment of the selection of her parents and children was still a traumatic issue for her ('I cannot liberate myself from this moment. I still suffer from insomnia today', Part I, 1h31min). However, the formulations show that, fifty years after the events, these tribulations troubled her exclusively on an emotional and psychological level; for her, they no longer played out in explicitly moral, let alone legal terms. In 1998, she was able to immediately balance her self-reproach with the praise she remembered from her mother: 'You always think about others'. Her main concern in the written account had been her own public moral and societal positioning, but at the time of the second account, she felt that she had convincingly addressed any lingering doubts in this respect through her more than thirty years of educational work, beginning with the foundation of her library in 1962.

In the different versions of her book, Olga Lengyel directs her attention towards Nazi perpetrators for four main reasons, which are her cultural background, her medical profession and her fascination with beauty as well as with power. The first aspect I want to explore is the proximity of the Hungarian language and culture and of the Transylvanian place of origin. Cultural prejudice and previous experience had predisposed Lengyel to a positive view of (ethnic) Germans in general. This applies to the camp doctor Fritz Klein and the camp pharmacist Victor Capesius. She categorises Klein as a 'correct assassin' (Lengyel 2000, 163). In the French edition of her book, she devotes a separate chapter under that title to Klein (Lengyel 1946, 226–228), revealing his obvious importance to her. In the English edition, she rather assembles several perpetrators in one chapter, titled 'The Beasts of Auschwitz', conveniently borrowing a catchphrase from contemporary British press reports. Journalists in the mid-1940s dubbed Josef Kramer 'The Beast of Belsen' and named Irma Grese as his female counterpart (Jaiser 2011, 341). Obviously, between the 1946 French edition and the 1947 English publication, there is already a transition from a more personalised approach to perpetrators to a group portrait with more general characteristics.

In the English version of the book, Lengyel describes herself as feeling personally indebted exclusively to Klein, who first chose her to become a liaison for the prisoner doctors after she had barely escaped selection to be killed in the gas chamber. Even if that might not be factual, it illustrates Lengyel's view of Klein to whom she even attributes 'nice manners' in that context (Lengyel 2000, 73). It is a telling example of what Dachau and Auschwitz survivor Hermann Langbein wrote about Auschwitz, namely, that any good deed had a much greater chance of remaining in people's memories than did the myriad incidents of harassment and torment. Auschwitz and Dachau survivor Ella Lingens seconded, 'Everyone who was there also did something good for once' (Langbein and Zohn 2004, 371), however, she also cautioned against letting a single action define a perpetrator's character or exculpate their overall behaviour. In Lengyel's Shoah Foundation interview, however, Klein was the only SS member she still remembers in all the complexity she had previously attributed to him (Part I, 2h25min). She vividly recalls in great detail how the block elder of her barrack had made her aware of Klein as a fellow Transylvanian from Brasov which triggered fond memories of her own visits to relatives in the city and of her own audacious approach to him, allegedly in order to obtain help for fellow prisoners (Part I, 2h28min).

The fact that Olga Lengyel then took over one of the coveted functions that the SS assigned to individual prisoners contributed significantly to her survival but also made her potentially vulnerable to criticism from her fellow inmates, thus weighing on her credentials as a victim. From then on, she operated within the manipulative power structure of the so-called prisoner self-administration built up by the SS. Immediately after the war, the debate among survivors on how to judge the actions and behaviour of former prisoner functionaries was ongoing. In the Belsen trial, twelve of the forty-five accused individuals had been prisoner functionaries whose verdicts ranged from acquittal to imprisonment for life, revealing the broad scope of verdicts that were passed to judge their actions in the camp. In the American military court trials at Dachau between 1945 and

1948, in every major trial on concentration camp atrocities, prisoner functionaries were also among the accused. While numerous former fellow inmates testified against them, there were also voices among survivors arguing that one could not measure them against the same yardstick as members of the SS.

It is difficult to imagine that Olga Lengyel was not aware of these debates; therefore, she probably also felt the need to use her memoir as a means of moral positioning. In this respect, fellow Auschwitz survivor Gisella Perl, a prisoner doctor who wrote her memoir around the same time as Lengyel while also residing in Paris, might have served as a reference for her, as Sheila E. Jelen argues in her chapter in this book. Both had been forced to work in the sick bay for female Jewish inmates in the camp area for Hungarian women at Birkenau. Perl's own disputed status is articulated in journalist and Holocaust researcher Ernst Klee's assessment of her actions as a 'prisoner coworker of Mengele' (Klee 2018, 312). However, although historian Andrea Rudorff acknowledges that Perl had had frequent contact with notorious camp physician Josef Mengele, she insists that Perl had never worked in his laboratories. She had, nevertheless, been forced to provide aborted foetuses for experimental purposes (Rudorff 2020, 24).

In Lengyel's written account, the manner in which she took up the work in the camp infirmary is presented in a way that appears to be beyond reproach. Her own initiative towards working as a prisoner nurse was allegedly rejected. Instead, she was 'chosen', 'sought out' and 'acted upon an order' and was then 'ordered' (Lengyel 2000, 69). The English and French versions correspond very closely in this aspect, with one notable deviation: In *Souvenirs de l'au-delà*, the opportunity for Lengyel to become a prisoner nurse resulted from the initiative of both camp doctors, Klein and Mengele (Lengyel 1946, 95). However, in *Five Chimneys*, Mengele is omitted, although their respective medical roles in Birkenau at the time suggest that his inclusion in the description in *Souvenirs* was most likely factual. For the American public in 1947, Lengyel obviously wanted to leave no doubt that Josef Mengele, from her point of view, was the complete moral 'other' who could not be credited with any positive effect for her. At the same time, Klein was still receiving a benevolently mixed reception from her.

Even in the Shoah Foundation interview, Lengyel's presentation of Klein remains full of ambiguity, when she recalls that he once publicly referred to her by name in the camp, something that was otherwise unheard of (Part I, 2h38min). Other survivors provided a more straight-forward assessment of his behaviour in Auschwitz-Birkenau. Ella Lingens repeatedly referred to him as a 'rabid anti-Semite' (Lingens and Lingens 2003, 131, 177 and 248)[4] and testified in the Frankfurt/Main Court in 1964, where the first large West German Auschwitz trial was held, that 'Klein ... was simply happy when he saw the smoke [of the crematorium] rising' (Tonbandmitschnitt des 1. Frankfurter Auschwitz-Prozesses 1964, 4). Accordingly, during an interview in 1974, she voiced her surprise after reading *Five Chimneys* that Olga Lengyel was still 'speaking highly of Dr Klein' (Lingens 1974, 00:35:41 h), allegedly even referring to him as 'the colleague from Klausenburg'. Auschwitz survivor and former prisoner doctor, Miklós Nyiszli did not mince his words either, calling Klein 'one of the evil, bloody-handed KZ officials' (Nyiszli 2012, 147), while Hermann Langbein singled out Lengyel as the only person known to him with an unusually positive view of Klein (Langbein and Zohn 2004, 397). As far as Josef Mengele was concerned, in her 1972 witness questioning during the Frankfurt/Main prosecution's investigation procedure against him, Lengyel also upheld her completely negative views of him. While she admitted that she did not personally witness him carrying out any human experiments, she explicitly incriminated him with shooting inmates, conducting selections for the gas chambers and reported from hearsay her knowledge of Mengele's alleged X-ray experiments with Polish nuns (Völklein 1999, 21, 136 and 165).

When it came to camp pharmacist Victor Capesius, Olga Lengyel's perception of him was on the whole sober and reserved, although he—like Klein—shared her ethnic German, Hungarian-speaking Transylvanian background. Like Gisella Perl, Lengyel claimed to have known him before her deportation when he was still representing the German pharmaceutical company Bayer in his native region and had liaised with local doctors and pharmacists. Despite their personal acquaintance, she insisted on having firmly dismissed his offers to help her relatives in late 1944 as sinister attempts to save his own skin, citing that '(e)xperience had taught (her) always to be wary of "benevolence" from these Nazis' (Lengyel 2000, 166). Capesius, too, left more pronounced impressions on other prisoners. Langbein succinctly summarised, '(h)e had a calming effect

---

[4] In the earlier English version, which differs substantially in content and was solely authored by Ella Lingens-Reiner under the title 'Prisoners of Fear' in 1948, Klein is referred to less often but equally explicit.

during selections, enriched himself and bribed prisoners' (Langbein and Zohn 2004, 397). Auschwitz and Dachau survivor Ladislaus Deutsch, whose mother was sent to the gas chamber by Capesius, while his disabled brother, who later perished in the Melk concentration camp, was spared, wrote: 'It is always remarkable when murderers behave humanely' (Ervin-Deutsch 2006, 213).

In the 1960s, Capesius briefly made newspaper headlines in West Germany, with reports about his particularly hideous deception of deportees. Based on Auschwitz, Sachsenhausen and Dachau survivor Mauritius Berner's testimony before the Frankfurt/Main court in 1964, reports were about how Capesius had sent Berner's wife and three children to the gas chamber, while overseeing the selection at the ramp in Birkenau on 29 May 1944 (Knellessen 2005, 2). In the 1960s, greater numbers of survivors were again heading into courtrooms, especially in West Germany, to testify against their former tormentors. West German society had eventually acknowledged the still existing need to judicially come to terms with crimes committed during Nazi rule, in particular, in Eastern Europe. Momentous change in the view of perpetrators was taking shape in those years. Raul Hilberg's comprehensive analysis of the Holocaust widened the scope of culpable participation in the Nazi regime far beyond the alleged pathological killers (Hilberg 2003), while Hannah Arendt tried to unravel the still widely accepted formula of 'perpetrator as demon' (Arendt 2006). And by acknowledging decently dressed middle-aged German men with respectable post-war careers walking as defendants into the courtrooms of the big concentration camp trials, the equation of Nazi perpetrators with lower-class thugs became less and less tenable in mainstream society.

In 1959, a new print run of the English version of Olga Lengyel's book was obviously underway, given that she added a dedication to it dated that year. There, she clarifies her mission as remembering her dead relatives as well as speaking up for those who were murdered in the camps. That same year, she reached out to US society at large by feeding small bits of her memoir to a popular men's war story magazine, where they were spiced up with salacious images. The story transported Lengyel's long-held view of perpetrators, as it showed wardress Irma Grese with the inaccurate caption 'Head of the women's camp, ..., looked like (an) angel but was vain, arrogant' (Lengyel 1959). Fritz Klein, however, was again introduced in a complex way as 'chief SS doctor, had to O.K. inmates for gassing, once saved 31 women from death'. Soon thereafter, the discourse on perpetrators would take the dramatic turn mentioned above. For the time being, however, Lengyel was content to simply perpetuate and publicise her view of her former tormentors from the immediate post-war years.

The second aspect that aroused Olga Lengyel's interest in perpetrators was her own medical professional background as a surgical nurse. It again brought Klein but also Josef Mengele to her attention. In 1947, she condemned the medical experiments at Auschwitz as having 'no scientific benefit' and being just 'cruel games'. In the earlier French edition of her book, the assessment is again less dramatic, calling them 'childish pleasures' and 'a fabric of contradictions' (Lengyel 1946, 245).[5] Her evaluation was based on purported scientific grounds, which were inaccurate, though. She had apparently transferred her focus on Mengele's interference with her idea of morals to the field of medicine here. For Lengyel, somebody as immoral as Josef Mengele could not possibly conduct proper scientific experiments.

However, while his experiments were conducted in unethical, criminal and consciously life-threatening ways, Mengele's studies on twins and anomalies in human development were backed at the time by highly respected, internationally renowned German research institutions. The cold water and salt water experiments that Lengyel wrongly transferred from Dachau to Auschwitz were guided by very rational and practical purposes to address common risks faced mainly by German Air Force soldiers. Mengele's acclaimed biographer David Marwell summarised that he belonged to 'the scientific vanguard [of his time and was] fully embedded in the contemporary medical mainstream' in Germany (University of California TV—The Library Channel [University of California Television (UCTV) 2021]). Lengyel's thinking about scientific experiments was not only factually misguided but even had an apologetic air about it, as if she wanted to defend the prisoner doctors who were forced to participate in them, probably with her deceased husband in mind who himself had been a prisoner doctor. She reasons that '[t]he men who had to conduct them [medical experiments] might have been able to excuse themselves could they have believed that they were at least serving science' (Lengyel 2000, 185). In the Shoah Foundation interview, she somewhat moderates her morally charged views on medical

---

[5] Wherever the French edition of Olga Lengyel's book is cited in English, it is my translation.

experiments: 'I don't know what these experiments meant at all', calling them a 'crazy... idea ... for persecution' (Part I, 2h53min). Over the decades, scientific research into the medical crimes of National Socialism has moved beyond reflecting on the alleged moral dilemmas in which the doctors working under the Nazi regime may have found themselves and has instead come to describe Nazi doctors as a functional elite dedicated to exploiting the opportunities offered by the regime. Lengyel, on the other hand, changed her assessment from seeing medical experiments as a particularly sinister crime to regarding them as just another means of persecution.

The third aspect of Olga Lengyel's engagement with perpetrators is her fascination with beauty, which makes her take an interest (again) in Josef Mengele and especially in Irma Griese (sic. Lengyel kept misspelling her name—Grese—throughout the various editions of her book). Their actions completely inverted Lengyel's understanding of the equation of beauty and morality. The underlying moral scrutiny of her own existence in the camp is informed by the conventional classical idea of taking beauty as a sign of being good in a moral sense. She obviously felt particularly disturbed by the notorious perpetrators Josef Mengele and Irma Grese, who fundamentally contradicted this ancient Greek ideal. To safeguard her moral bearings, she kept applying this standard to herself as a camp inmate, as well, when she repeatedly noted how unfavourably her own dress and appearance compared to those of Irma Grese and Fritz Klein (Lengyel 1946, 159 and 230). The dismay resulting from this perceived moral inversion is expressed through an almost obsessive engagement especially with Grese's and Mengele's outer appearance and actions.

In another incident recounted in the English version where death and survival were closely entwined, Olga Lengyel accredits Irma Grese with sparing her life once because Grese had allegedly been curious about what Klein had to do with Lengyel (Lengyel 2000, 103). There, she presents Grese as someone who had power over her, possessed beauty and chose beauty when it came to selecting aides from among the prisoners for her pleasure, only to cruelly condemn them to extermination once she had lost interest in them or felt they might compromise her status. Thus, Lengyel's moral imagination seems to have been completely inverted by Grese, as well, to the point that, for Lengyel, in Auschwitz beauty might even have become a sign of amorality. This essential recalibration of her moral compass also seems to have guided her self-view. At one point, she realises the profoundly negative impact Grese's power had on her and her fellow inmates, leading her to the confession that 'the Germans succeeded in making murderers of us' (Lengyel 2000, 114). This acknowledgement, in turn, triggers Lengyel's 'violent hatred' of Grese (Lengyel 2000, 160). Grese, in particular, challenged Lengyel's moral standards in yet another way because as a woman, with her violent and cruel behaviour, she also transgressed against the established order of the sexes. Here, Lengyel's judgement oscillates between outrage and blatant voyeurism (esp. Lengyel 2000, 160–162).

In the 1998 interview, the humiliation Lengyel had felt about the miserable rags prisoners were clad with was still palpable ('this feeling hurt me much more than the ... fact that I was cold', Part I, 1h41min). However, by then her concern about perpetrators' morally corrupt beauty had significantly receded. At one point in the interview, she cannot even remember Mengele by name anymore and after being prompted by the interviewer, refers to him just as 'a fanatic, ... a very handsome man' (Part I, 2h24min). And about Irma Grese, she can only recall having seen her photo in a newspaper and later discovering her in footage of the Belsen trial she had watched in Paris in 1945 (Part I, 2h44min). Over time, Lengyel seems to have lost her apparent negative fascination with Nazi perpetrators and eased the sense of moral degradation she experienced at Auschwitz-Birkenau and which she later projected onto them.

In addition to the deep impression Grese's alleged beauty left on Olga Lengyel and many of her fellow inmates, Grese also caught the eye and captured the imagination of numerous international journalists at the Belsen trial (Langbein and Zohn 2004, 448). It was mainly their coverage and Grese's appearance on photos and in newsreels that created her image as the 'beautiful beast', which Lengyel would also cite in the English version of her book. Research into Allied Nazi crimes trials has shown how media coverage already early on produced the image of the sexually deviant, abnormal female perpetrator (Weckel and Wolfrum 2003, 16). In contrast, survivors' witness evidence during the trial largely consisted of matter-of-fact statements about when, where and how Grese had mistreated inmates. The sexually charged perception of Grese thus is, at least partly, an effect of media coverage and of survivors' memoirs such as those from Olga Lengyel and Gisella Perl. Similarly sexually charged representations of Grese can also be found in other Auschwitz survivors' accounts, notably those by Krystyna Zywulska, Fania Fenelon and Isabella Leitner (Jaiser 2011, 339 and 346). Last but not least, West German courts' perception (and judgements) of female Nazi perpetrators also enhanced the image of 'exceptional "female brutes" [...] with unbridled sexuality' (Szejnmann 2008, 30–31). Thereby, the judiciary also contributed to attempts from within society at comfortably distancing itself from Nazi atrocities by othering those who were responsible for them.

Furthermore, Olga Lengyel's view of sexuality as an expression of moral order becomes obvious in the English edition's chapter 'Love in the Shadow of the Crematory' (Lengyel 2000, 195–203). There, she sounds very much like Gisella Perl, who opines in her account that the victims died 'to satisfy the sadistic instincts of those perverts' while recalling that female inmates had to undress in front of 'abnormally sexually excited SS men' (Perl 2020, 55 and 69). Over several pages, Lengyel indulges in sexually charged gossip about the alleged adventures of Irma Grese (Lengyel 2000, 160–162). Here, Perl complements this mindset by presenting Grese as 'one of the most beautiful women' and 'a sexual pervert' (Perl 2020, 87) while framing her comments with the revenge fantasies she harbours in connection with Grese. Lengyel even draws an immediate connection between crimes and sexual behaviour when answering her own rhetorical question: 'Who can forgive them [perpetrators] all the crimes they committed? The Griese (sic) woman was bisexual. My friend, who was her maid, informed me that Irma Griese frequently had homosexual relationships with inmates and then ordered the victims to the crematory' (Lengyel 2000, 199). Immediately after liberation, she expressed her own impressions of and fantasies about Irma Grese in ways that also shaped contemporary societal perceptions, discourses, and representations in the media.

Perl's and Lengyel's texts as accounts by well-known female survivors often appear in gender-historical debates on concentration camps, which also results from their emphasis on the alleged sexual-pathological deviance of the perpetrators and Perl's professional background as a gynaecologist. This emphasis is usually combined with references to Grese (Gelbin 2013).[6] Olga Lengyel also denounces German barrack leaders as having a 'high percentage of homosexuals and other perverts', while musing about people from Georgia as being 'a race said to produce the handsomest men' (Lengyel 2000, 201). Her language becomes more refined in the 1998 Shoah Foundation interview, where she talks about

---

[6] On this aspect, I benefited from exchanges with Sebastian Paul.

homosexual men and women—after a brief pause, apparently searching for the right words—as 'men who liked men, women who liked women' (Part I, 2h04min). She might just have adopted the changes within contemporary social discourse or, indeed, rid herself of prejudice in line with her redeveloped identity as an educational entrepreneur.

An essential part of Lengyel's idea of moral order—and the fourth link to perpetrators—was her fascination with power which allowed the Birkenau camp commandant Josef Kramer to catch her attention. She describes her first encounter with Kramer as 'looking at a cobra' and later attributed 'a Buddha-like air' (Lengyel 2000, 84 and 153) to him. This certainly tells us more about Lengyel's impression of the Buddha than anything about Kramer but also, indirectly, about her view of power relations. At the end of her book, this is neatly summed up in her assessment of the plight of slaves in ancient Egypt 'who built the pyramids and died (having seen) the work of their hands rising always' (Lengyel 2000, 228), thereby attributing positive meaning to allow them to reconcile with their exploitation. Again, a negative fascination with cold power shines through. And Lengyel concedes to this force a capacity to comfort its victims as long as they are allowed to contribute to a higher goal, revealing the power structure inherent to her moral standards in the mid-1940s.

Finally, in an incident that once more highlights the close entanglement between the biographical accounts of Olga Lengyel and Gisella Perl, a temporary inversion of the power structure of the concentration camp is presented. Both claim to have been involved in an abortion allegedly performed on Irma Grese (Lengyel 2000, 162) but they exclude each other from the scene in their respective accounts. However, this overlapping claim also speaks to the strength of their individual moral imaginations wanting to overcome what they perceived as the power of absolute evil, especially in Birkenau.

Conclusion

After Auschwitz-Birkenau, the perpetrators served as a negative foil for Olga Lengyel to reflect on her own social and moral positioning. Lengyel declared that everyone who had been involved with Nazi crimes should be punished, but when it comes to her main concern with morality she formulates that 'The Germans have sinned grievously but so have the rest of the nations' (Lengyel 2000, 227), leading her towards general moral reflections on whether 'man [is] good or bad'. This mirrors her ambiguous judgement of Fritz Klein, who, on the one hand, 'merited capital punishment a hundred times' but also left her with 'the impression that he, too, was a victim of circumstance' (Lengyel 2000, 163). In her 1998 interview, the moral ambiguity is clearly compartmentalised into two opposite poles. On the one hand, Lengyel articulates sentimentality about her common Transylvanian roots with Klein (Part I, 2h28min) and on the other, she voices 'satisfaction' (Part I, 2h46min) about having seen a picture of Klein being forced to bury corpses of dead inmates of Bergen-Belsen in a newspaper.

Olga Lengyel's 1947 memoir was both influenced by and fed into a developing discourse on perpetrators who allegedly had either behaved like animals or stayed decent even when participating in crimes. This looks like an uncanny continuity of the self-image of the SS, which had also officially insisted on their members' 'decency' while at the same time nominally condemning those who inflicted 'unnecessary cruelty' on their victims. This 'decency', of course, meant doing one's duty within the terror system and only harassing the victims according to the rules, which in practice were often exceeded by limitless violence and arbitrariness. In 1948, Ella Lingens acknowledged the impact of the media and the over-simplification of the image of SS perpetrators. She herself had insisted on a more differentiated image of perpetrators in her own memoir but had admonished at the same time that 'it is right and just that it has been drawn in precisely those outlines, to be shown to young people and be kept before their eyes as the incarnation of evil, a perpetual warning and an abomination' (Lingens-Reiner 1948, 129).

Olga Lengyel assessed her imprisonment as a trial of her capacity to act morally. She saw herself and others under the threat of being 'reduced to the lowest moral level', before reassuring her readers that 'one required an extraordinary moral force' to 'cling to their human dignity to the very end' (Lengyel 2000, 228–229), only indirectly implying that she herself belonged to that group. However, when the Shoah Foundation inter-viewer prods her in 1998 with the question 'How does the Holocaust impact on your life today?', in her reply, she openly displays renewed moral reassurance and self-confidence: 'I never could do anything else but doing something that it should not be repeated' (Part II, 0h57min).

In her 1946/47 memoirs, Olga Lengyel tries to adjust her moral bear-ings after undergoing their temporary reversal in the concentration camp. Evaluating alleged acts and behaviours of perpetrators was a tool used in this process. Looking through the lens of *Five Chimneys*, it becomes clear that Lengyel ascribes to someone like Fritz Klein the potential to combine the binary poles of good and evil within one person. Thus, she is able to still relate to him within a shared moral universe even five decades later. On the contrary, Grese and Mengele epitomise, for Lengyel, absolute evil in the morally 'topsy-turvy world' of Auschwitz-Birkenau and, thus, have to be demonised and banned from the common sphere of morality. However, in her 1998 interview, she emphasises her life before and after her ordeal at Auschwitz and her renewed self-confidence in a retrieved moral agency no longer challenged or unsettled by her troubling memories of Auschwitz. In 1947, she looked at Auschwitz as a major adversity she was only just able to overcome. By then, she was still caught up in the magnitude of the struggle she had had to go through. Fifty years later, she could look back on a mastered past that she had successfully turned into an educational tale to be retold for posterity's sake.

REFERENCES

Arendt, Hannah. 2006. *Eichmann in Jerusalem: A Report on the Banality of Evil*. Penguin Classics. New York, NY: Penguin Books.

Ervin-Deutsch, Ladislaus. 2006. Ein letztes Zeugnis - Mein Fall Capesius. *Dachauer Hefte, Realität, Metapher, Symbol: Auseinandersetzung Mit Dem Konzentrationslager* 22: 208–213.

Gelbin, Cathy. 2013. 'Gender and Sexuality in Women Survivors' Personal Narratives'. In *Representing Auschwitz: At the Margins of Testimony*, edited by Nicholas Chare and Dominic Williams, 174–93. Palgrave Macmillan Ltd. https://research.manchester.ac.uk/en/publications/gender-and-sexuality-in-women-survivors-personal-narratives.

Hilberg, Raul. 2003. *The Destruction of the European Jews*. New Haven, Conn.: Yale University Press.

Jaiser, Constanze. 2011. 'Irma Grese (1923–1945). Zur Rezeption einer SS-Aufseherin'. In *Im Gefolge der SS: Aufseherinnen des Frauen-KZ Ravensbrück: Begleitband zur Ausstellung*, edited by Simone Erpel and Mahn- und Gedenkstätte Ravensbrück, 2. Aufl, 338–46. Schriftenreihe der Stiftung Brandenburgische Gedenkstätten 17. Berlin: Metropol-Verl.

Klee, Ernst. 2018. *Auschwitz: Täter, Gehilfen, Opfer und was aus ihnen wurde: ein Personenlexikon*. 1. Auflage. Fischer Taschenbuch 19785. Frankfurt am Main: Fischer Taschenbuch.

Knellessen, Dagi. 2005. 'International Forced Labour Documentation Project (IFLDP). Protocol of the interview with Kornelia Berner, Jerusalem'. Archiv Deutsches Gedächtnis, Hagen University.

Kogon, Eugen. 2023. *Der SS-Staat: das System der deutschen Konzentrationslager.* Genehmigte, ungekürzte Ausgabe. München: Wilhelm Heyne Verlag.

Langbein, Hermann, and Harry Zohn. 2004. *People in Auschwitz.* Chapel Hill: The University of North Carolina Press.

Lengyel, Olga. 1946. *Souvenirs de l'au-delà.* Translated by Ladislas Gara. Paris: Éditions du Bateau Ivre.

Lengyel, Olga. 1959. 'Camp of Captive Women'. *For Men Only* 6 (11): 12–15, 54.

Lengyel, Olga. 2000. *Five Chimneys: A Woman Survivor's True Story of Auschwitz.* Chicago, IL: Academy Chicago Publ.

Lingens, Ella. 1974. United States Holocaust Memorial Museum collection - interview with Ella LingensAudio. United States Holocaust Memorial Museum. https://collections.ushmm.org/search/catalog/irn516248.

Lingens, Ella, and Peter-Michael Lingens. 2003. *Gefangene Der Angst: Ein Leben Im Zeichen Des Widerstandes.* Wien: Deuticke.

Lingens-Reiner, Ella. 1948. *Prisoners of Fear.* London: Victor Gollancz.

Matthäus, Jürgen. 2005. 'Historiography and the Perpetrators of the Holocaust'. In *The Historiography of the Holocaust,* edited by Dan Stone, Nachdr., 197–215. Basingstoke, Hampshire: Palgrave Macmillan.

Nyiszli, Miklos. 2012. *Auschwitz: A Doctor's Eyewitness Account.* Translated by Richard Sevear and Tibere Kremer. 1st edition. Penguin Classics.

Perl, Gisella. 2020. *Ich war eine Ärztin in Auschwitz.* Edited by Andrea Rudorff. Translated by Klaudia Ruschkowski. Wiesbaden: Marix Verlag.

Reitlinger, Gerald. 1981. *The SS, Alibi of a Nation 1922–1945.* 2nd Edition with a new foreword by Martin Gilbert. Englewood Cliffs, N.J: Arms & Armour Press.

Rudorff, Andrea. 2020. 'Einführung in die deutsche Ausgabe'. In *Ich war eine Ärztin in Auschwitz,* by Gisella Perl, 6–36. Wiesbaden: Marix Verlag.

Szejnmann, Claus-Christian. 2008. *Perpetrators of the Holocaust: A Historiography.* Loughborough University. https://repository.lboro.ac.uk/articles/chapter/Perpetrators_of_the_Holocaust_a_historiography/9469826/1.

'Tonbandmitschnitt des 1. Frankfurter Auschwitz-Prozesses'. 1964. 1964. https://www.auschwitz-prozess.de/zeugenaussagen/Lingens-Ella/.

University of California Television (UCTV), dir. 2021. *Mengele: Unmasking the 'Angel of Death' with David Marwell.* https://www.youtube.com/watch?v=0Fybz7VJ4-8.

Völklein, Ulrich. 1999. *Josef Mengele: Der Arzt von Auschwitz.* 1. Aufl. Göttingen: Steidl.

Weckel, Ulrike, and Edgar Wolfrum. 2003. 'NS-Prozesse und ihre öffentliche Resonanz aus geschlechtergeschichtlicher Perspektive'. In *'Bestien' und 'Befehlsempfänger'. Frauen und Männer in NS-Prozessen nach 1945: Frauen und Männer in NS-Prozessen nach 1945*, edited by Edgar Wolfrum and Ulrike Weckel, 1st edition, 9–21. Göttingen: Vandenhoeck & Ruprecht.

CHAPTER 6

Epilogue

Peter Davies, Hannah Holtschneider, Sheila E. Jelen,
and Christoph Thonfeld

Abstract The epilogue considers Lawrence Langer's 2021 critique of
Lengyel's testimony and its place in Holocaust scholarship in light of
the insights gained in the preceding chapters about narrative, translation, publication contexts, morality and gender. Challenges about the
veracity of aspects of Lengyel's accounts, we contend, need to be considered in relation to the multi-disciplinary study of testimonial statements
of Holocaust survivors. We posit the value of detailed engagement with
'embellished' Holocaust testimonies (Sue Vice) and propose to read
historical inaccuracies in relation to the narrative strategies, publication
contexts and addressees of the testimonial statements.

Keywords Lawrence Langer · Truth · Embellished testimonies ·
Narrative

This book is the product of several years of discussion between the four
scholars represented here and a number of interlocutors. From the very
beginning, we were confronted by a challenge that has shaped our work in
ways that we were not expecting when we began. One of those interlocutors expressed serious doubts about the veracity of Lengyel's testimony
and shared, with the rest of us, an essay by Lawrence Langer, which

© The Author(s), under exclusive license to Springer Nature
Switzerland AG 2025
P. Davies et al., *Olga Lengyel, Auschwitz Survivor*,
https://doi.org/10.1007/978-3-031-82490-6_6

sought to debunk Lengyel's story. In his 2021 essay, titled 'Memory and Invention in Olga Lengyel's *Five Chimneys*', Langer enumerates different ways in which Lengyel's testimonies, both written and audio-visual, cross from fact into mediocre fiction. He points out that a number of improbable events that Lengyel reports as factual make her text seem untrustworthy and, thus, potentially open the door for discourses of denial that are based on inaccuracies in Holocaust testimonies. Lengyel's depiction of an abortion in Auschwitz allegedly performed on Irma Grese has been exploited by Holocaust deniers due to the discrepancies it shows compared to the way Gisella Perl described allegedly the same scene in her memoir. Deniers use such contradictions in reports of former concentration camp inmates to discredit survivors' accounts altogether. Grese, in particular, has become a key figure for Holocaust deniers' attempts to 'clear her name' by utilising any minor discrepancies in survivors' accounts to dismiss their value as evidence. This might have been one of the reasons why Lawrence Langer so acrimoniously attacked Lengyel's memoir for its factual deficiencies.

Another twist in the problematic relationship of Lengyel's biographical accounts with truthfulness and factuality is highlighted by Sue Vice (Vice 2014). She traces intertextual connections between *Five Chimneys* and a book by Australian Bernard Brougham in which he falsely claimed to have been a Holocaust survivor named Bernard Holstein (Holstein 2004). There she shows how the author obviously adapted motifs of Lengyel's account (including the cold water experiments, which Lengyel erroneously relocated from Dachau to Auschwitz) to claim them as his own experiences. Citing this example, Vice goes on to classify Lengyel's 'embellished testimony' as a 'well known [...] [site] of literary borrowing' (Vice 2014, 186), that is, Lengyel's account becomes part of the discursive evolution of Holocaust literature and is thus indirectly corroborated by being adopted across genres and by different authors as an authenticating reference. In her essay, Vice also highlights Lawrence Langer's status as a whistleblower against false Holocaust testimony, as he had publicly voiced doubts about Misha Defonseca's alleged survivor account (Defonseca et al. 2005) when it became widely known in Europe and the United States in 2007, which contributed to an evaluation process in which it was subsequently revealed to be untrue.

Langer's main problem with Lengyel, in the final analysis, is threefold. First, he resents the fact that Lengyel refuses to acknowledge that she is a Jew and that she was deported to Auschwitz like all the other Jews from Kolozsvár/Cluj. She insists, according to Langer, on maintaining her uniqueness and agency and thus cannot allow herself to be swallowed up in the narrative of Hungarian Jewry, either during their deportation or in the camp. Langer's second issue, built on the first, is that Lengyel tells a story of life in Auschwitz that obfuscates its very essence, which is that those who were imprisoned there were stripped of their uniqueness, their identity and their humanity. Instead, Lengyel tells an unlikely story about her ability to move relatively freely about the camp, to interact with SS officials, and to maintain her identity to such an extent that she is called by name during a roll call. Langer's concern, in this account, is not that Lengyel seems to be 'embellishing', which is a common feature of memory texts of all kinds, but that she is misrepresenting the experience of Auschwitz in a way that he believes will undermine the accepted understanding of its psychological terror (Langer 2021, 176). Of this, he says: 'in Lengyel's narrative we are faced repeatedly not with examples of "false memory", but of "faked" memory. The majority of her counterfactual episodes are designed not to explore the abysses of Auschwitz', he says, 'but to enhance her own stature' (Langer 2021, 194). Langer's third, and final major concern resides in what he understands to be scholarly negligence in encounters with Lengyel's testimonies. He opens his essay with the following statement: 'no one has taken the trouble to question its accuracy or analyse its embellishments'. To this day Albert Einstein's tribute to the author is often cited on the book's cover: 'You have done a real service by letting the ones who are now silent and most forgotten speak' (Langer 2021, 169). While Einstein is not exactly a scholar of the Holocaust, Langer does accuse other illustrious scholars whose work is much closer to the subject, such as Tzvetan Todorov and Robert Eaglestone, of being uncritical and sloppy in their approaches to Lengyel's work (Langer 2021, 171).

Langer, who died on 29 January 2024, was a scholar of literature and a model for scholars interested in understanding ways to approach Holocaust testimonies from outside of a strictly historical perspective. His trailblazing book, *Holocaust Testimonies: The Ruins of Memory* (Langer 1993), closely read testimonies in the Yale University Fortunoff Video Archive for Holocaust Testimonies and sought to parse the differences between literary testimonies and audiovisual ones. Additionally, his work on French non-Jewish Auschwitz survivor Charlotte Delbo's trilogy, *Auschwitz and After* (Delbo 2014), demonstrated Langer's sensitivity to the tenuous nature of memory with his distinction between what he sees as the way she depicts both 'deep' memory and 'common' memory. Deep memory, according to Langer, is the mode of representing memory of the trauma from within the traumatised self while common memory is the way trauma is represented in terms that are comprehensible to those who are accustomed to normative rules of social and discursive engagement (Langer 1993, 1–38). In other words, deep memory is a memory that cannot be expressed in terms that others will fully be able to engage, memories of profound thirst, of deadly hunger and of the drive to survive at the expense of anything and everything in the surrounding environment, including fellow prisoners. Common memory, on the other hand, is a memory that has been processed and adapted for public consumption; it is a memory that can be tolerated by those living outside the 'concentrationary universe' (Rousset 1946), those whose sense of propriety is still intact and who would be hard pressed to fully comprehend the kinds of compromises imposed upon those living within the concentrationary universe itself, either in the past or in the psychological present.

Attuned, due to his literary training, to the nuances of representation and its intersection with memory and culture, one would expect Langer to approach Lengyel's 1946 testimony not only with a more sophisticated literary lens but also with more empathy. Why does he valorise Charlotte Delbo's explicit articulation of the way that her thirst and her hunger distorted her memory and impacted her ability to recount her experiences while excoriating Lengyel for her lapses in memory?

Writing right after the war, Lengyel sought to convey truths and facts about the experiences she had undergone. The post-war trials were going on, and her initial testimony, a memoir, strove for artlessness and for historical evidence. Lengyel, unlike Delbo, was not aware of the limitations of her own perception, and to some extent, as we have explored in the chapters of this book, she borrows others' stories in order to craft what she views as a more comprehensive approach to the experience of Auschwitz (we recall the claim made by the subtitle of the earliest English edition of *Five Chimneys: The Story of Auschwitz*). While Delbo points out her own lapses in memory, Lengyel does not. And perhaps this is what fundamentally irks Langer. With a more attentive literary lens, however, Langer might have reconsidered his harsh critique.

As Peter Davies argues in his discussion of translation, Lengyel finds herself between testimonial genres, straddling the historical, the judicial and the personal in her writing style and her explicitly stated goals for the text. For Langer, it seems, Lengyel has left the literary behind, and he no longer uses literary tools to evaluate her work. Rather, he implies that the contract she establishes with her reader is a historical one. Calling her story a memoir, but attempting to tell stories that are not her own, lamenting her own personal trauma but couching it in terms of collective experiences such as the underground and the Jewish women's infirmary in Auschwitz-Birkenau, her work, for Langer, is not only inauthentic, but dangerous. How dangerous? Dangerous in the face of Holocaust revisionism, in the face of those who seek to disprove the details of Holocaust narratives so they can demonstrate that the whole event was a hoax.

This is, of course, fully justified by Langer's concern that *Five Chimneys* might provide ammunition for Holocaust denial. However, he is also taking issue with Lengyel's account in other respects. By citing obvious factual errors taken over from Lengyel's book by literary scholar Tzvetan Todorov in his study *Facing the Extreme: Moral Life in the Concentration Camps* (Todorov 1997), Langer actually targets Lengyel's moral-oriented assessment of Auschwitz through his critique of Todorov. For Langer, undermining Lengyel's credibility not only serves the purpose of defending other survivors' testimonial trustworthiness but also allows him to score a few points in the struggle for interpretational authority over life in the Nazi camps.

What seems to bother Langer most is that these 'improbable episodes' were used by Lengyel 'to celebrate the ingenuity and the agency of [their] protagonists' (Langer 2021, 176), which goes against Langer's and others' proposition of widespread loss of control over one's fate, of the loss of individuality and identity in the camps. However, what Lengyel first and foremost tried to achieve was 'to maintain her narrative and figurative control not over her fate, but over the narration of her experiences', as Hannah Holtschneider points out in her chapter in this book.

Consequently, it is not so much the questionable factuality of Lengyel's account of Auschwitz that is at stake, but rather the narrative re-framing of her experiences at Auschwitz in ethical terms that are designed to preserve a particular self-image. Especially in the case of Olga Lengyel's frequent alleged encounters with notorious Nazi perpetrators, Langer simply dismisses them as expressions of her preposterous claim to a degree of agency even as a prisoner at Auschwitz. On the contrary, Lengyel rather applies SS officers and guards as foils to herself so she can reassure herself of having retained moral integrity even in Auschwitz-Birkenau. What is more, frequently referring to Nazi criminals who could be seen in news coverage internationally also served Lengyel as a means of authentication for her account in the immediate post-war era.

Langer's central thesis about testimony suggests that any redemptive elements negate the absolute ruin signified by the Holocaust and are, therefore, giving a 'false' account of the reality of the experiences. This effectively removes survivor agency from the narrative or rather, only permits it in the telling of what can be established as historical fact, but not in assigning meaning to experiences. His 2021 chapter on Lengyel does the same: where Lengyel assumes and takes agency, Langer criticises her for allegedly giving 'false testimony', because she embellishes, invents and moralises.

In part, Lawrence Langer's challenge to her veracity has stimulated our close scrutiny of Lengyel's testimonies. We are grateful to him for his reading of it and are also pleased to be continuing his legacy of close engagement with Holocaust testimonies. Even if we are not in full agreement with his conclusions in the particular case of Olga Lengyel, trying to better understand why he was so alarmed by her account in *Five Chimneys* has proven invaluably generative to us as we imagine future directions for approaching testimonies from interdisciplinary perspectives. In our discussions, we have found that Langer's essay stimulates thought, but also potentially forecloses other productive approaches. There is a risk of imposing an interpretation before engaging constructively and critically with the text on its own terms.

There have been challenges to Langer's view of agency in recent Holocaust historiography: for example, Hájková (2021, 6) contends that Langer's critique of the 'moralization of life in the death camps' leads him to deny the prisoners any agency, and argues that 'dismissing prisoners' agency because their actions were only rarely "successful" – that is, because they did not survive – is an erringly linear view'. Further, we bring together insights from historiographical and literary studies in order to think differently about the narrative functions of agency in Lengyel's testimonies. In our view, Langer's 'character assassination' of Lengyel effectively silences her agency, which is central to her testimonial narrative and sense of self: it is almost as if the deprivation of agency in the historical events themselves is mirrored and reinforced in Langer's condemnation of Lengyel. By contrast, we are interested in *how* Lengyel claims agency and we seek to read her embellishments as meaningful beyond their literal meaning. Indeed, questions of agency and identity that are negotiated in concentration camp testimonies have as much to do with the context, conditions and language(s) in which the testimony is written or spoken as with the conditions in the camp itself. Through our diachronic approach to Olga Lengyel's testimonies, we have been able to point out how the different historical and social circumstances and respective targeted audiences have impacted her narrative.

While Langer was a key figure in the establishment of norms around the academic treatment of Holocaust testimonies and we are indebted to him for bringing to our attention some of the infelicities to be found in Lengyel's 1946 book, we are eager to move beyond concerns about Holocaust denial that may cloud critical judgement and force critics to discredit 'inaccuracies'. Dori Laub in *Testimony* (Laub 1992, 59–60) famously describes a woman testifying about the Auschwitz rebellion in exaggerated terms, claiming that multiple crematoria were blown up when we know that only one was partially destroyed. A group of historians listening to her felt that they must discard the entirety of her testimony. Laub reminds us that the experience of rebellion in Auschwitz was so unimaginable, so fabulous and boundary-breaking that he is not surprised at her exaggerated memory. Indeed, he argues, perhaps her faulty memory tells a story that a historically accurate one could not have told, namely the story of the *experience* of rebellion at Auschwitz from the perspective of a bystander who was not expecting it and processed it as a sensational shattering of the concentrationary universe:

> The woman was testifying [...] not to the number of the chimneys blown up, but to something else, more radical, more crucial: the reality of an unimaginable occurrence. One chimney blown up in Auschwitz was as incredible as four. The number mattered less than the fact of the occurrence. The event itself was almost inconceivable. The woman testified to an event that broke the all compelling frame of Auschwitz, where Jewish armed revolts just did not happen, and had no place. She testified to the breakage of a framework. That was historical truth. (Laub 1992, 60)

Like Laub, we are interested not necessarily in what Lengyel gets wrong, but in why Lengyel tells her story the way she does and what that teaches us about Holocaust testimony; we are interested in ways of reading it and understanding it both in its own moment and as the discourse shifts over time.

In March 2024, all four of the scholars represented in this volume led a session of Hannah's class 'The Holocaust in History and Culture' at the University of Edinburgh. Students had been asked to read Olga Lengyel's *Five Chimneys* as well as Lawrence Langer's essay about it. We asked the students to share their thoughts on Lengyel's book and, strikingly, they pointed out many features of the narrative that we have been discussing for several years and that are reflected in our respective essays. One student said that it sounded like Lengyel's writings were 'based on others' writings'. In fact, Sheila's essay suggests that Olga Lengyel might be speaking for the female collective, and recapitulating stories told by other women in positions of some power in the camp, like Gisella Perl. Another student observed that Lengyel's book is very 'busy', exhaustingly busy in fact, and contrasted her style to Elie Wiesel's, which they characterised as much more meditative and calming despite its horrific content. In Peter's essay on translation, he addresses this 'busyness' by suggesting that Lengyel uncomfortably straddles several genres (testimony, autobiography, reportage), perhaps because the text was written so soon after the war when a literary discourse on the Holocaust had yet to be established, and she was situated at a cultural crossroads, between Hungary and France.

In a similar vein, a third student suggested that it is important to read 'between the lines' of Lengyel's embellishments in order better to understand what the embellishments themselves might tell us. Echoing Christoph's essay, they surmised that Lengyel may have been tuned into some of the ongoing post-war trials and may have been interested in addressing the culpable complicity of inmates and enforced participation in medical crimes that were being negotiated in court. Finally, someone else asked about the way that Lengyel seems to promote the idea of Auschwitz's survivability, tapping into Langer's criticism of Lengyel's representation of Auschwitz as a place where it was possible to maintain dignity. This was reminiscent of Hannah's discussion of the challenges to the authenticity of Lengyel's text brought about by her claims to authority and agency.

In light of the fact that this volume is designed also to be a teaching tool, we were gratified to see, in the course of the class discussion, that the issues we have touched upon in our essays were at the forefront of these students' readings. Certain Holocaust texts are particularly evocative in the classroom because of the ways in which they reflect controversies and complexity within the discourse of Holocaust representation. Elie Wiesel's *Night* (Wiesel 2006a, b) taught within the context of its shift from Yiddish to French and from a Jewish to a largely non-Jewish European audience is one of those texts. Why and how, in the same texts in different languages, did the rage directed by Wiesel at Germans in the Yiddish shift, in the French and all subsequent translations from it, to a rage at God (see Seidman 1996; Davies 2018)? At what historical juncture were different audiences ready to read such a text, and in what terms? How does translation not only render a text accessible to different audiences but also render a text palatable for different audiences?

Binjamin Wilkomirski's false testimony *Fragments* (Wilkomirski 1997) is another one of those eminently teachable texts. At what point do we need to suspend our disbelief in the memories of survivors who were too young to make any linear sense of their experiences, and at what point do we call them liars? To what extent have Holocaust tropes been adopted by the culture to the point of becoming kitsch?

Olga Lengyel's *Five Chimneys*, in its early articulation of a woman's experience in Auschwitz-Birkenau, of a mother's loss of her children, her parents and her spouse in one fell swoop, of an assimilated Hungarian Jew caught up in the maw of the systematic antisemitic mass murder, is worthy of study on its own terms. Furthermore, essential aspects of our diachronic reading of Lengyel's testimonies like the evolution of discourses and genres, shifts in narrative emphases, accentuating some memories while downplaying and harmonising others and over time blanking out some entirely, will provide fruitful points of departure for future classroom discussions of testimony. Our work on Lengyel's testimonies situates them at a productive nexus of considerations about the nature and the value of Holocaust testimony which will continue to inspire critical yet empathic engagement with it.

REFERENCES

Davies, Peter. 2018. *Witness between Languages: The Translation of Holocaust Testimonies in Context*. Rochester, NY: Camden House.

Defonseca, Misha, Vera Lee, Marie-Thérèse. Cuny, and Sue Rose. 2005. *Surviving with Wolves: The Most Extraordinary Story of World War II*. London: Portrait.

Delbo, Charlotte. 2014. *Auschwitz and After. Translated by Rosette C. Lamont*, 2nd ed. New Haven, Connecticut: Yale University Press.

Hájková, Anna. 2021. *The Last Ghetto*. An Everyday History of Theresienstadt: Oxford University Press.

Holstein, Bernard. 2004. *Stolen Soul*. Australia: Judy Shorrock: distributed by UWA Press.

Langer, Lawrence. 1993. *Holocaust Testimonies: The Ruins of Memory*. New Haven: Yale University Press.

Langer, Lawrence. 2021. 'Memory and Invention in Olga Lengyel's Five Chimneys'. In *The Afterdeath of the Holocaust*, 169–95. Cham: Springer International Publishing.

Laub, Dori. 1992. Bearing Witness or the Vicissitudes of Listening. In *Testimony: Crises of Witnessing in Literature, Psychoanalysis, and History*, ed. Shoshana Felman and Dori Laub, 57–74. New York, NY: Routledge.

Rousset, David. 1946. *L'univers Concentrationnaire*. Paris: Éditions du Pavois.

Seidman, Naomi. 1996. Elie Wiesel and the Scandal of Jewish Rage. *Jewish Social Studies* 3 (1): 1–19.

Todorov, Tzvetan. 1997. *Facing The Extreme: Moral Life in the Concentration Camps*. Reprint. New York, NY: Henry Holt & Co.

Vice, Sue. 2014. 'False and Embellished Holocaust Testimony'. In *Textual Deceptions: False Memoirs and Literary Hoaxes in the Contemporary Era*, by Sue Vice, 142–202. Edinburgh University Press. https://doi.org/10.3366/edinburgh/9780748675555.001.0001.

Wiesel, Elie. 2006. *La nuit*. Edited by François Mauriac. Double 42. Paris: les Éd. de Minuit.

Wiesel, Elie. 2006. *Night*. Edited by Marion Wiesel. 1. ed. of this translation. New York: Hill and Wang.

Wilkomirski, Binjamin. 1997. *Fragments: Memories of a Childhood, 1939–1948*. London: Picador.

Author Index

SUBJECT INDEX

The manufacturer's authorised representative in the EU is Springer
Nature Customer Service Centre GmbH, Europaplatz 3, 69115 Heidelberg,
Germany. If you have any concerns regarding our products, please
contact ProductSafety@springernature.com

Printed and bound by CPI Group (UK) Ltd, Croydon, CR0 4YY

29/04/2026

02099450-0012